The
Person and Work
of the Holy Spirit
in the life of the believer

The
Person and Work
of the Holy Spirit
in the life of the believer

GEORGE B. DUNCAN

15368

JOHN KNOX PRESS
ATLANTA

This book is dedicated with gratitude and affection to all those members and friends of St. George's-Tron Church who by their faithful presence and prayers made the giving of these Bible Studies possible in the mercy and goodness of God.

Library of Congress Cataloging in Publication Data

Duncan, George B
    The person and work of the Holy Spirit in the life
of the believer.

    Reprint of the 1973 ed. published by Lakeland, London.
    1. Holy Spirit.   I. Title.
BT121.D86 1975   231'.3   74-21900
ISBN 0-8042-0681-3

1975
Printed in the United States
John Knox Press
Atlanta, Georgia

Contents

Foreword

by Canon A. T. Houghton

In these days when there is so much interest in the subject of the Holy Spirit, especially on the part of young Christians, the Rev. George Duncan gives in these Bible addresses the positive and clear teaching which is greatly needed to dispel current confusion of thought on this topic.

Written from the heart, and faithful to the Word of God, this book is in the true tradition of Keswick teaching as it has been proclaimed down the years, and which remains as relevant as ever to the needs of today. It is a privilege to commend it wholeheartedly, with the prayer that the Lord will graciously use it in blessing to many.

A.T.H.

Introduction

The following chapters consist mainly of notes of Bible-studies on "The Person and Work of the Holy Spirit in the Life of the Believer" given in my own mid-week fellowship of prayer and Bible-study at St. George's-Tron Church in Glasgow.

I felt constrained to take up this subject in view of the current confusion in language, in thought and in understanding about the person and work of the Holy Spirit.

These studies have also appeared in the *Life of Faith* and it is in response to a demand to have them made available in a more permanent form that I have agreed that they should be published.

Everyone, surely, is agreed that we desperately need to see evidences in our lives, individually and corporately, of the power of the Holy Spirit. It is with the earnest hope and prayer that these studies may help to clarify people's thinking and direct their experience into the fulness which is part of the plan and purpose of God for His Church, and through His Church for the world. If these studies succeed in helping Christians to a right understanding of the person and work of the blessed Spirit Himself, then I shall feel the studies have not been published in vain.

I would acknowledge gratefully my debt to writers and commentaries whose names will be quoted in the studies and whose thoughts have been an inspiration to me.

It will rapidly become clear that I do not write as a theologian or as a scholar but simply as a minister of the Gospel who seeks to make plain the word and truth of God to the ordinary believers, that great community of Christian folk who make up the bulk of our congregations and who are the backbone and strength of the Church of Christ universal.

1 The Divine Personality of the Holy Spirit

In all our consideration of the Holy Spirit our minds are to be governed, our thoughts are to be guided, by the fact that we are thinking in terms of a relationship between two persons; between the personality of the Divine Spirit and the personality of the redeemed sinner.

It is interesting to note that three of the books I consulted for this first study begin with the personality of the Holy Spirit. Bishop Handley Moule, the saintly scholar and bishop, in his book on the Holy Spirit entitled *Veni Creator* and in the chapter on the Holy Spirit in his other book entitled *Outlines of Christian Doctrine* begins with this aspect of the divine personality in each case. Dr. Campbell Morgan, one of the greatest Bible expositors who has ever lived, begins part one of his book *The Spirit of God* with a chapter on "The Personality of the Holy Spirit." Dr. R. A. Torrey, again, devotes the first chapter of his book *The Holy Spirit* to the same theme.

When we consider that we are to think in terms of a relationship between personalities, we find that there are three crucial areas of thought which need to be kept prominently in our minds. The first is:
A. *Attitudes are crucial in the matter of relationships between personalities.* If the relationship is going to be right, then the attitudes must be right. Surely we can say with confidence that the attitude of the Holy Spirit will

1

always be right. The danger of a wrong attitude will lie always with ourselves and a failure in our attitude can lay us open to two possible blunders.

The first blunder is:

(i) *The blunder of thinking that we can make use of the Holy Spirit.* The only possible attitude between a redeemed sinner and the Divine Person of the Holy Spirit is not "How can I use Him?" but "How could He use me?" If I think of the Holy Spirit as an influence, then maybe I could control that influence just as I might control the wind, channelling its power and using it for my own ends. But if the Holy Spirit is a *Divine Person* I must not even begin to think of using Him. And yet so often this is precisely the blunder that we make; so often we want to have the presence and power of the Holy Spirit for purposes of our own, so that we may be more effective in our Christian service, so that we may be delivered from our sins and failures! But the moment you and I start trying to use the Holy Spirit there will be trouble. The Holy Spirit, this Divine Person, is not someone to be ordered about at my behest to suit my convenience, to further my ends. He is the *Divine* Spirit, the Spirit *of God* and I am but a redeemed sinner. We dare not, we must not, stand above the Holy Spirit and look down on Him, telling Him what He must do for us, what He must be in us, what He must give to us.

The second blunder is:

(ii) *The blunder of thinking we can have more or less of the Holy Spirit.* You cannot have more or less of a person. You either have a person or you do not. You can have more or less of a person's trust or confidence, which will mean that person will share more with you of what he has or less with you of what he has and is. The determining

2

factor will not be with him but with you. There is always a conditioning element in relationships between personalities. Surely there is no unwillingness on the part of God the Holy Spirit but there may well be an unpreparedness, an unfitness on our part which puts a brake upon the outgoing of the Holy Spirit in all that He is and wants to be to us, in us and through us.

The Bible tells us that the Holy Spirit is the gift of God to every sinner who has seen his need of Christ and who has trusted Christ to meet that need. This is made abundantly plain in Acts 2:38 where we are told that the Holy Spirit comes to men as a "gift." But the Holy Spirit that has been given to us can be grieved by us (Ephesians 4:30) and the grieving of the Holy Spirit is always the result of a wrong attitude on our part.

How often this can happen in human relationships: where there should be openness and confidence there can creep in reserve and uncertainty and doubt. The attitudes between two personalities somewhere or other has gone wrong and someone or something has been the cause of it. So we need to remember that a relationship between personalities has to do essentially and crucially with *attitudes*.

But this relationship has to do with more and so we need to recognize that:

B. *Activities are crucial in the matter of relationships between personalities.* People do things, by deed or thought or word, and all the activities of the Holy Spirit in the Word of God are those that demand personality to put them into effect. The activities of the Holy Spirit, as recorded in Scripture, are the activities of a person. So there are two questions we have to ask concerning the activities of the Holy Spirit which He is recorded as

3

having carried out and therefore which we would assume He would want to carry out in and through our lives.

(i) *What has been recorded of His activities?* We hear again and again that the Holy Spirit "speaks." Only a person can speak. When Philip had gone from Samaria to the south and the chariot of the Ethiopian Eunuch came along, we read, "the Spirit said unto Philip, Go near, and join thyself to this chariot" (Acts 8:29). After Peter's vision upon the housetop we read, "the Spirit said unto him, Behold, three men seek thee" (Acts 10:19). Again and again the record tells us that the Spirit of God speaks to men—only a person could do that. Compare Acts 13:2 where Saul and Barnabas were sent out. Then at the end of each of the letters to the seven Churches in the Book of the Revelation we are told: "He that hath an ear, let him hear what the Spirit saith unto the churches." The Holy Spirit, therefore, is Someone who speaks.

The Holy Spirit is also Someone who teaches. In John 14:17 He is called by Christ "the Spirit of truth" and in verse 26 our Lord says, "He shall teach you all things." In chapter 16:13 we read "He will guide you into all truth." Paul takes this up in 1 Corinthians 2:10 where he reminds the intellectually arrogant Corinthians that there is a world of the Spirit to be explored and understood, that there is in fact a university of spiritual knowledge where the Holy Spirit fulfils the role of Teacher. He describes it in verse 6 of that chapter as "not the wisdom of this world" and in verses 9 and 10 he writes, "Eye hath not seen, nor ear heard, neither have entered into the heart of man, the things which God hath prepared for them that love him. But God hath revealed them unto us by his Spirit: for the Spirit searcheth all things, yea, the deep things of God." He speaks! He teaches! And only a person can teach and speak.

The Holy Spirit, we are told, "prays." The Revised Standard Version translation of Romans 8:26 reads, "the Spirit helps us in our weakness; for we do not know how to pray as we ought, but the Spirit himself intercedes for us with sighs too deep for words." Bishop Handley Moule suggests that this is something the Holy Spirit does in and through the believer. He speaks! He teaches! He prays! Surely only a person can pray.

The Holy Spirit "leads." We are told in Romans 8:14 (RSV) that "All who are led by the Spirit of God are sons of God." With divine wisdom He leads us through all the bewildering experiences of life. Amid all the clamour of men's voices His voice will be heard. He leads us as a person would lead. He is the One who was named by Christ as "the Comforter"—the Paraclete; the One called alongside to help. And just as the disciples followed the Saviour, so they were to follow their Divine Guide—the Holy Spirit.

These are just some of the recorded activities of the Holy Spirit. They could only be those of a living personality. This raises the other question:

(ii) *How must I relate to His activities?* The answer is surely a simple one. I must be willing to allow Him to fulfil these activities still. Does He speak? Then I must listen. Does He teach? Then I must be willing to learn. Does He pray? Then I must be found on my knees. Does He guide? Then I must follow and obey.

In human relationships the activities of any personality can be selfish, or they can be stupid, or they can be sinful. Maybe we have to say in human relationships that certain activities must cease. But that could never be so

5

with the Holy Spirit. Divine wisdom, love and power are His and I must be willing to allow this divine person to do what He wants to do, in me, with me and through me.

So the relationship between the personality of the Divine Spirit and the redeemed sinner has to do with *attitudes*, with *activities*, and finally:

C. *Attributes are crucial in the matter of relationships between personalities.* I have to take into account not simply what a person does but who and what a person is. This, of course, lies behind what he does and is the character of the person. I have to consider more than what a person may give or say, and I have to ask what kind of person he or she is. This is something I need to know before I relate to a person in friendship. What they do may be pleasant; what they say may be interesting; what they give may be generous; where they go may be delightful; but behind all that, what kind of persons are they? My dictionary tells me that "attribute" means "that which is inherent in, inseparable from"; that which, in other words, a person is. What kind of a person is the Holy Spirit?

Here we need to find out:

(i) *The kind of personality He has.* That He is a person is already clear. He is Someone who knows. Compare 1 Corinthians 2:11 where Paul writes "the things of God knoweth no man, but the Spirit of God." He is Someone who wills: He has intention—see 1 Corinthians 12:11. In that great chapter in which Paul deals so authoritatively with the gifts of the Spirit, he writes of the absolute sovereignty of the Holy Spirit who divides and distributes these gifts, or withholds them "to every man severally as He will." He is Someone who thinks. In Romans 8:27 Paul refers to "the mind of the Spirit." What thoughts

He must have about you and—about me! He is Someone who loves. Paul writes of "the love of the Spirit" in Romans 15:30. The love of God the Father is a thought with which we are familiar; the love of Christ the Son is another thought with which we are familiar. How many of us stop to think of the love of the Spirit?

But who is He—this One who knows, who wills, who thinks, who loves? What He is can be deduced, of course, from the names given to Him in the Bible, which always reflect the character. Ephesians 4:30 tells us that He is "The Holy Spirit" and therefore we must associate holiness with Him. Romans 8:14 says He is "the Spirit of God" so I must never lose my sense of awe and worship and wonder, for He is not only holy He is divine. In John 14:16 and 17 our Lord calls him "the Spirit of truth" so there is absolutely no trace of falsehood or insincerity to be found in Him. Romans 8:9 tells us that He is "the Spirit of Christ," therefore His character is that of Christ Himself. 2 Corinthians 4:13 says He is "the Spirit of faith" or faithfulness—He is someone who is completely and utterly reliable. This, then, is that kind of personality the Holy Spirit has and is. And therefore I have to face the second thought:

(ii) *The blend of personality He seeks.* In the great prayer of Christ in John 17:21 our Lord prays, "that they may be one in us." In Matthew 19:5 we read the purpose of marriage is that "the two shall become one." What is the goal, therefore, in this relationship between the personality of the Holy Spirit and my personality? Surely, it is simply this—that what I do should be what He would do; that where I go should be where He would go; that why I serve and how I serve should be why and how He would serve.

7

The ultimate fulfilment of the person and work of the Holy Spirit is, of course, the fruit of the Spirit. We read of that in Galatians 5:22. And when the fruit of the Spirit is being shown in my life then it simply means that the blend of personality is perfect and complete.

So let us think through these three tremendous facts about the relationship between myself and this divine person:

> The importance of Attitudes;
> The importance of Activities;
> The importance of Attributes.

Ch. 1 Holy Spirit is a person

2 The Gifts of the Holy Spirit

1 CORINTHIANS 12

We now move on to consider what we are calling "the gifts of the Holy Spirit"—not "the gift" of the Holy Spirit which Peter speaks of in Acts 2:38 as being part of the experience of conversion and not a second kind of experience. The choice of the word "gift" here sheds light upon *the way* in which the Holy Spirit comes to us—He comes as a gift. I cannot buy a gift; I do not deserve such a gift; but He comes to me as God's gift.

The "gifts" of the Holy Spirit, however, differ from the "gift" of the Holy Spirit in that they refer to gifts of abilities, of capacities that the Christian will and does receive from the Holy Spirit and it is worth noting that the Bible tells us these are gifts in which *every* Christian has a share. Not that every Christian will have every gift but that each Christian will have at least one gift. No Christian will be "gift-less." Compare 1 Corinthians 12:7 and 11.

This makes nonsense of a phrase that has become current in our day. People speak about the "charismatic movement" or the "charismatic gifts" as if these words described some Christians but not all. The word "charismatic" is derived from the Greek word "charisma" meaning "gift" or "free gift" and *every* born-again believer has been given one gift or another. Every Christian, therefore, is a "charismatic Christian," that is, a gifted Christian. To use this word as it is being used today is to create the sense of division within the Church which is the very last thing the Holy Spirit intends to do: to use it as it is used by some today is to create two kinds of Christians, whereas the Bible knows basically only one. What these folk who use this word really mean is that some Christians who have experienced but one of the gifts of the Holy Spirit, namely that of speaking in tongues, can somehow regard themselves as being in some strange way different, better than, further on than, other Christians who have equally received one or more of the charisma—the gifts—but *different* gifts.

I want therefore to turn with you to the passage in 1 Corinthians 12, which is the classic passage in which Paul deals with this whole question, a passage in which he begins by saying that he wanted to dispel their ignorance in the matter. May I remind you of the vital importance of taking the Word of God, and not the experience of men, as the grounds for what we believe and of what we therefore bear witness to—truth which is divine, not experience which can be human. This is the foundation of our faith. I want us to note:

A. *The diversity experienced concerning the gifts of the Spirit.* Right away we face a head-on collision between the teaching of Scripture and the teaching of some Christians. How often I have met Christians who want to impose a uniformity where the Word of God has laid down the principle of diversity. They say that unless you have one particular gift, that being the gift of tongues, either you cannot be a Christian or you cannot be one who is filled with the Spirit. Listen to what the Bible says here: in verses 4, 5 and 6 the word comes again and again —diversity, diversity, diversity— and in verses 8 to 10 the same sense of diversity is stressed—"to one is given,"

10

"to another," "to another," "to another." The whole section ends with a series of rhetorical questions to which the implied answer is "No" (verses 29 and 30). "Are all apostles?" No! "Are all prophets?" No! "Are all teachers?" No! "Are all workers of miracles?" No! "Have all the gifts of healing?" No! "Do all speak with tongues?" No! "Do all interpret?" No! And where the Bible says ' "No" I dare not, I must not, say "Yes."

There are two thoughts underlying this principle of diversity:

(i) *The unity from which this diversity is derived.* That unity is, of course, the unity of the one Spirit. There are many gifts, many abilities, but *one* Spirit: and so two other words run alongside the words "diversity" and "another," and they are the words "the same" and the word "one." Underlying all the diversity of capacities and abilities which are the gifts of the Holy Spirit, gifts in which every Christian has a share, is the living presence of this one blessed Divine Person.

Not so long ago we went south to be with our family. We stayed in the home of our son John with Jennie, his wife, their two little boys, George and Timothy, and Lisa, the Finnish au pair girl. We took gifts with us—their Christmas gifts: to John it was a shirt; Jennie and Lisa each had a length of material with which to make dresses; to George and Timothy we gave Fair Isle hats and gloves of different sizes and the toys "Tom" and "Jerry." Suppose we had insisted that they all had the same gift, say, the little bendable Jerry. They had us, of course, and our presence was something that they all experienced but beyond ourselves we brought gifts for each one of them individually and these gifts were

11

different. Our gifts, of course, were designed mainly for their pleasure but served other purposes besides.

So it is with the Holy Spirit. He gives us first of all Himself and then to each a gift—one gift at least—for not a single Christian is without some gift.

(ii) *The authority by which this diversity is decreed.* The choice of the gifts is not mine, nor is it the choice of other Christians, it is the choice of God the Holy Spirit. Look at the way Paul stresses this again and again. In verse 8 he emphasizes that the gifts are *given to* us not *chosen by* us. In verse 11 he tells us "*the Spirit divides* to every man severally *as he* (the Holy Spirit) *will.*" To *every* man (to each man, individually) as *He* will. Again in verse 18, "*now hath God set* the members every one of them in the body, as it hath pleased Him," not as it hath pleased me or my friends or some creature but "as it hath pleased *Him.*" And again in verse 28 the same authority is described. In the face of this I just cannot understand how Christians who take the Word of God as their authority in matters of faith or conduct can ever tell any other Christians that they ought to have, that they must have, one particular gift. God never contradicts Himself and to state that this or that gift is an essential is to contradict God and that is a dangerous thing for anyone to do. Which gift is given to which person is for God the Holy Spirit to decree and not for man.

As well as the diversity experienced, I see here:
B. *The absurdity exposed.* The absurdity with which Paul now deals is in the first place heard in:

(i) *The way some Christians talk.* In verse 15 we read, "If the foot shall *say*"; in verse 21 we read, "the eye cannot *say.*" In the first instance Paul deals with the absurd way in which people can talk just because they do *not* possess certain gifts. They are so discouraged and the absurdity lies in their *discouragement*; and they become discouraged usually because of the foolish talk of some other Christians who make them feel that they are not really Christians at all, or that they are not proper Christians, that somehow or other God therefore cannot use them. Paul says, in effect, "don't be so absurd, don't be so stupid" and he deals with this in verses 15 to 20. "Because I can't speak like so-and-so, I am no use." This is precisely the terrible absurd situation that can arise when some misguided and ignorant Christians say to others that if you don't have one particular gift (and as at Corinth it is always the same gift—the gift of tongues) then there is something wrong, something lacking.

Others talk equally stupidly against a background, not of discouragement, but of disparagement—the disparagement of Christians who, in their judgment, are less spiritual, less gifted! Paul says again, "don't be so silly." In verse 21 he says, "the eye cannot say to the hand, I have no need of thee: nor again the head to the feet, I have no need of you."

Here are two exceedingly stupid ways of talking; one by Christians who have been made to think that because they don't have a particular gift they are no use, that they might just as well not be Christians; and the other stupid way of talking is to speak about these very people as if what they said was true. Discouragement and disparagement shows itself in the way some Christians talk.

The other absurdity exposed is found in:

(ii) *The way some Christians think*. From verse 22 we have the whole question of evaluation. Paul points out that in the physical body some of the most important functions are carried out by the least attractive members; their functional value is much more important than their physical appearance. A girl may have a beautiful face but it will soon be much more important to her husband that she can cook a decent meal!

We see this in society: the people who keep our streets tidy are really of much greater importance than the pop singers who fill our screens, and yet we admire the one and despise the other!

So it can happen in the matter of the gifts of the Spirit. The person who has one special gift could be tempted to look rather pityingly upon the Christian who has not! Paul says, in effect, "God has in the physical creation of our body attributed a vital importance to organs which do not particularly impress the observer with their beauty." I have never yet heard anybody say about a beautiful girl, "Hasn't she got a beautiful liver or kidneys?" But without a liver or kidneys, beautiful or not, she could not live! And so in the body of the Church, essential and important gifts are being exercised yet evoke no comment, get no publicity, arouse no envy, and yet without them the work of the Church would grind to a halt tomorrow. The tragedy is that these very Christians are sometimes despised as inferior!

C. *The identity expressed.* The whole question of the gifts of the Spirit is set within the context of the Church as the body of Christ. These gifts are never treated as simply something concerning me as an individual but as something relating to other Christians and to Christ. They are given "to profit" and the profit is not my own personal profit but the profit of the whole fellowship of other Christians. In verse 12 and following, Paul uses the illustration of the body—one body with many members—and in verse 27 he makes the final declaration "ye are the body of Christ, and members in particular."

This conception of the Church, the living Church, of those born again of the Spirit of God and indwelt by the Spirit, is found elsewhere in the Epistles. Compare Ephesians 5:23 and Colossians 1:18 where Paul sets out Christ as being "the head of the body, the church." If Christians are to be regarded as different members of the body of Christ, and if each different member of the body has its different function to perform, we can see what the ultimate purpose of the gifts of the Spirit really is. Surely it is the same as when the varying members of a healthy body carry out their own functions and yet carry them out in relation to all the other members and in co-operation, in collaboration, and in harmony with them!

This leaves us with two tremendous thoughts. For what purpose does the body exist? What is the significance of the body to the living personality who inhabits the physical frame? The first thought, for me, concerns:

(i) *The person that will be seen through the body.* It is through the body that personality expresses itself and reveals itself. If there is love, then, that will be expressed through the body by the words on the lips, the look in the eye, the touch of the hand. So where each member of the body of Christ is functioning, using the gift that God has given, Christ's person will be seen. It will take all the gifts of all of us to reveal Him completely and perfectly.

The second thought is:

(ii) *The purpose that will be served by the body.* And the purpose is not my purpose but His. That little jingle of words expresses a profound truth:

He has no hands but our hands to do His work today:

15

He has no feet but our feet to lead men in His way:
He has no voice but our voice to tell men how He died:
He has no help but our help to lead them to His side.

The ultimate work of the Holy Spirit is to testify of Christ and to glorify Christ, and Christ is glorified when His person is seen, when His purposes are served and His will done. The real and final work of the Holy Spirit is to bring us to Christ and to bring Christ to us, then through us to bring Christ, and reveal Him, to the world.

The identity expressed by means of the gifts of the Holy Spirit functioning healthily, functioning harmoniously is the identity of Christ expressed in and through His body, the various members of the body, the Church.

3 The Baptism with the Holy Spirit

ACTS 1:1–14

In this study I want to begin by stressing the importance of vocabulary. A great deal of confusion, I believe, is caused by failure on the part of many Christians to use the terminology of the Bible.

It is important to remember that every sport, every profession, every art has its own vocabulary and if we participate in any of these there is no good getting impatient about the need for accuracy in the use of words. The surgeon presumably has a name for every different kind of instrument that he uses and it is no use the nurse saying, "I will call this instrument what I like." If she attempts that kind of looseness of language and definition she will soon find that the surgeon starts calling *her* what he likes and she won't appreciate that! The conductor of an orchestra has a name for each of the instruments in the orchestra, and there is no use somebody coming along and saying, "It makes no difference to me what he calls the instruments, I have my own name for each of them. He may call one a flute but I am going to call it a cello." Likewise the plumber, like every other tradesman, has a name for each of his tools and they are recognized by their names. The golfer has a name for each of his clubs and there is no good his caddie saying, "I don't care what you call the clubs, I have names of my own." The result would be confusion, and so we could go on. Parents have names for each of their children and there is no good a stranger coming along and saying, "I don't care what you call your children, I have names of my own for them."

Names are important if we are going to avoid confusion and a disregard of this elementary fact by many Christians has produced complete confusion in the thinking of Christians concerning the person and work of the Holy Spirit and particularly what I am calling part of the initial experience of that Spirit, namely, the Baptism of the Holy Spirit.

We have already discovered that the manner in which we receive the person of the Holy Spirit is as a gift. He has been given to us by God, through Jesus Christ, in response to repentance and faith in Jesus Christ. This is made abundantly plain in Acts 2:38. The *manner* of the coming of the Holy Spirit into our lives is as "a gift"; the *meaning* of the coming of the Holy Spirit into our lives is, however, covered by the word "baptized with the Holy Spirit." I want us to examine this from three points of view:

A. *The promise made of the baptism of the Holy Spirit.* This promise was made:

(i) *At the commencement of the ministry of our Lord.* In the first instance, it was made by John the Baptist in his ministry and he made it to differentiate between his ministry and the coming ministry of Jesus Christ. It was made by John himself. We get references here in Matthew 3:4–11; Mark 1:6–8; Luke 3:16. They are familiar words and every Christian knows them: "I indeed baptize you with water . . . He shall baptize you with the Holy Ghost and with fire."

Here are statements made by John concerning the nature of the ministry of Jesus Christ; a ministry that was to affect all who came in faith to Him. He was not describing the ministry of our Lord while He was on earth but the ministry which He would exercise as a result of what His ministry on earth, His death and resurrection had made possible. In John 1:33 John tells us how this distinctive ministry of our Lord's had been revealed to him. "He that sent me to baptize with water, the same said unto me, 'Upon whom thou shalt see the Spirit descending, and remaining on him, the same is he that baptizeth with the Holy Ghost.' " It is interesting to note that here the tense used for "baptizeth" is a present tense; that is, the announcement made to John was one which revealed what was to be characteristic of the continual ministry of Christ; as I say, not on earth but after His resurrection and ascension.

Somebody has said, so truly, that Christ came not to preach the Gospel but that there might be a Gospel to preach, and part of that Gospel is that He does baptize with the Holy Ghost. So we see the promise made of the baptism of, or with, the Holy Spirit was made quite clearly at the commencement of the ministry of our Lord. We also see it made:

(ii) *At the conclusion of the ministry of our Lord.* The only other statement which promises the baptism of the Holy Spirit is one made by our Lord Himself in Acts 1:5. "John truly baptized with water; but ye shall be baptized with the Holy Ghost"—and then our Lord tells them when ... "not many days hence " That is to say, they would be baptized with the Holy Ghost on the day of Pentecost. And here again we note that this experience was promised to *all.* Our Lord did not say, "some of you will be baptized with the Holy Ghost." By implication, surely, He meant that all of them would be baptized with the Holy Ghost—'ye shall be baptized with the Holy Ghost not many days hence." There we have the promise made, and let us hold on to it, and it was made to all believers and made concerning a distinctive feature of the ministry of Jesus Christ.

B. *The problem raised by the Baptism of the Holy Spirit.* And the problem is a simple one. Was the baptism of the Holy Spirit a second experience in the lives of the disciples or was it a first experience of the coming of the Holy Spirit into their lives? Is it, therefore, a first or second experience for us? This is an absolutely crucial problem and one that we have to look at in the light of what the Scriptures say. Let us examine:

(i) *The experience of the disciples before Pentecost.* When you and I turn back to the teaching of Jesus Christ concerning the incoming or the indwelling of the Holy Spirit, all the language used by our Lord in His teaching to the disciples suggests that Pentecost and the baptism of the Holy Spirit was, in a very real sense, their *initial* experience. Listen to what Christ says. Earlier on in His ministry, in John 7:37 and 38 we read, "In the last day, that great day of the feast, Jesus stood and cried, saying, If any man thirst, let him come unto me, and drink. He that believeth on me . . . out of his belly shall flow rivers of living water." Then in verse 39 the comment is added, "But this spake he of the Spirit, which they that believe on him should receive: for *the Holy Ghost was not yet given*; because that Jesus was not yet glorified." Note that. This would seem to indicate that the experience of the Holy Spirit, that was in the purpose of Christ for all who believed in Him, was *not yet possible*.

Listen again to the Lord's words in the upper room discourse, where He has more to say about the person of the Holy Spirit than anywhere else. In John 14:16 He says, "I will pray the Father, and he shall give you another Comforter, that he may abide with you for ever;" in verse 17, "He dwelleth with you, and shall be in you." In verse 26 He says, "the Comforter . . . whom the Father will send . . . shall teach you all things"; and again in John 16:7, "It is expedient for you that I go away: for if I go not away, the Comforter will not come unto you; but if I depart, I will send him unto you." It would seem to me as if Christ is making it absolutely plain that whatever the disciples experienced of the Holy Spirit before Pentecost, they were not believers in the Christian sense of the word: they were not born again of the Spirit of God. They were believers in His Diety, of course they were. They had come to that conviction. But so is the Devil a believer in the Deity of our Lord. They were also believers in His Messiahship. We can see this right up to Acts 1:6 where, in the moments before the ascension, they were still thinking in terms of an earthly kingdom. You remember they asked the Lord saying, "Lord, wilt thou at this time restore again the kingdom to Israel?"

It is, however, quite clear from these verses in John 14 and 16 that our Lord is speaking of the indwelling of the Holy Spirit *as a future experience* but not as a present experience. This is precisely the position taken by Dr. Campbell Morgan, the great Bible expositor who exercised such a powerful ministry in Westminster Chapel for several decades. So we have to face up to this very real likelihood that the Lord's followers were disciples but they were not Christians in the full New Testament sense of the word; they were believers but not in the sense that a Christian today is a believer. And so we turn to:

(ii) *The experience of the disciples after Pentecost*, we find that the gift of the Holy Spirit, indwelling, transforming, filling and using the believer is something possible only after Pentecost. Do you recall how Peter speaks on that great day in Acts 2:32 and 33? "This Jesus hath God raised up, whereof we all are witnesses. Therefore being by the right hand of God exalted, and having received of the Father the promise of the Holy Ghost, he hath shed forth this, which ye now see and hear." Our Lord had said that the Holy Spirit was not yet given because Jesus was not yet glorified. Here, Peter would indicate that the Holy Spirit was poured out only after our Lord had been exalted and received of the Father. When was Jesus glorified? And therefore when was the Holy Spirit given? Our Lord was surely glorified when, having been crucified, He was raised from the dead, He ascended and was seated on the right hand of God the Father—there He is exalted and glorified! And it was only after the ascension, and therefore at Pentecost, that the Holy Spirit was given to *all* men who believed.

It is interesting to find in Acts 10 and 11 that Peter identifies in the conversion experience of Cornelius and his household the "gift of the Spirit" and the "baptism of the Spirit." In Acts 10:45 there is recorded the astonishment that fell on Peter and others that "on the Gentiles also was poured out the gift of the Holy Ghost." And in Acts 11:15–17 when Peter is recounting at Jerusalem what had happened at the home of Cornelius he says, "And as I began to speak, the Holy Ghost fell on them, as on us at the beginning. Then remembered I the word of the Lord, how that he said, John indeed baptized with water; but ye shall be baptized with the

Holy Ghost. Forasmuch then as God gave them the like gift as he did unto us, who believed on the Lord Jesus Christ; what was I that I could withstand God?" So in the mind of Peter, at least, in the conversion experience of Cornelius, the receiving of the gift of the Holy Spirit was to him something to be identified with the baptism of the Spirit as experienced by the disciples on the day of Pentecost.

And so we have this truth emerging which seems to me the inevitable deduction from what the Scripture has to say: the baptism of the Holy Spirit, which the disciples experienced on the day of Pentecost, was *not* a second experience of the Holy Spirit in their lives but a first and an initial experience of the Holy Spirit, which is described as far as its spiritual meaning is concerned as the baptism with the Holy Spirit.

C. *The purpose served through the Baptism of the Holy Spirit.* What does the baptism of the Holy Spirit achieve in Scripture? What purpose does it serve? We find in Scripture that it is associated with two tremendous truths. The first is with:

(i) *The body of Christ.* This scripture is found in 1 Corinthians 12:13 where Paul stresses again that the baptism in, or with the Holy Spirit is a baptism into the body of Christ, into one body. The word translated in the Authorized Version "*by* the Holy Ghost" in the Greek is the word "en"—exactly the same word as found in Matthew 3:11 and Acts 1:5. It is not a baptism *by* the Holy Spirit here and a baptism *by* Jesus Christ there; it is a baptism *with* the Holy Spirit *by* Christ. It is obvious that Paul here is referring to an *initial* experience and a *universal* one in which every Christian in the Corinthian Church had shared. He does not say that *some* of them

23

had been baptized with the Holy Spirit and others had not, but that they were *all* baptized—good, bad and indifferent Christians as they were. They had all been baptized with the Holy Spirit into one body and here the purpose is stated clearly—the baptism with the Holy Spirit is a baptism into one body, that is the body of Christ.

Now the purpose of the baptism with the Holy Spirit, in which all believers share at their conversion, is to bring us into, make us a living part of, the body of Christ. That one body, with its many members, is under the control of the One who is the head of the body, even Christ. The other purpose served by the baptism with the Holy Spirit in Scripture concerns not simply the body of Christ, or the true Church—the invisible Church—but it concerns:

(ii) *Our union with Christ.* The other scriptures which throw light upon the purpose and the meaning of the baptism with the Holy Spirit are found in passages like Romans 6:3 following, where St. Paul refers to the baptism with the Holy Spirit as being that experience by which we are brought into union with Christ. The baptism in Romans 6 is not water baptism—that would never do all that Romans 6 speaks about—it is the baptism with the Holy Spirit that brings us into *union with Christ* and enables us to share in everything that Christ experienced. And so, in Galatians 3:26 and 27 we read the same truth, "Ye are all the children of God by faith in Christ Jesus. For as many of you as have been baptized into Christ have put on Christ." And again, the baptism is not water baptism, it is a baptism with the Holy Spirit. In Ephesians 4:5 and 6, Paul speaks of, "One Lord, one faith, one baptism, One God and Father of all." And the one baptism is, of course, the baptism with the Holy Spirit.

The Christian in the New Testament is never told he *must* be baptized with the Holy Spirit; he is told that he *has been* baptized with the Holy Spirit. We never read in the New Testament that just *some* have been baptized with the Holy Spirit and others have not been baptized with the Holy Spirit, but we find that *all* have been baptized with the Spirit into the body of Christ, and brought into union with Him. The baptism with the Holy Spirit in the New Testament has to do with something that happened at conversion. It was the Holy Spirit uniting us to Christ, uniting us to one another and creating a living spiritual bond that has brought into existence a new living community. This is the body of Christ, through which the person of Christ will be seen and through which the purposes of Christ are to be served.

The baptism with the Holy Spirit in the New Testament is always an initial experience, it is always a universal experience, it is always a spiritual experience. We never read of a Christian *seeking* it but always of a Christian *sharing* it and sharing it with all other Christians. "You *will be* baptized with the Holy Ghost" is promised before Pentecost. "You *have been* baptized with the Holy Ghost" is recorded after Pentecost. Epistles and the Acts. Whatever fuller experience we may seek for ourselves it is not the baptism with the Holy Spirit. That there *are* fuller experiences I don't doubt for one minute, but please do not let us call any fuller experience the baptism with the Holy Spirit—that is simply creating confusion. In my reading of what the commentators have to say, one comment seemed to me enlightening. One commentator pointed out that until the baptism of John, no Jew was ever baptized—only proselytes from other nations and other faiths were baptized. For them, water baptism was part of their introduction to their new life in a new community, in a new faith. The baptism of the Holy Spirit in Scripture seems to be exactly that. It is that experience of the Holy Spirit which initiates us into a new community, into a new relationship with Christ, into a new relationship with other Christians when we become many members of the one body sharing the same life.

The baptism with the Holy Spirit, then, in the New Testament is an initial experience and a universal experience. It is never stated that some Christians have been baptized with the Holy Spirit but others have not. Let us stick to the language of Scripture and thus avoid confusion in our thinking or in our praying.

4 Be Filled with the Spirit

EPHESIANS 5:15–6:9

We now come to examine what is meant by being "filled with the Holy Spirit," or what is sometimes called "the fulness of the Holy Spirit." Bishop Handley Moule is careful to point out, however, that the phrase "the fulness of the Holy Spirit" is neither Pauline nor is it verbally biblical. Rather than talking about "the fulness of the Spirit," therefore, we will talk about being "filled with the Spirit."

I want us to note that this particular aspect of the person and work of the Holy Spirit is:

1. *Recorded of Christians* in Scripture. We will not take time here to consider references to being filled with the Spirit prior to Pentecost, where this was always associated with special people for special services. After Pentecost it is recorded both as an experience of "being filled" and as a conditional state of being "full." It is recorded both of groups and also of individuals. Similarly, the experience happened to the same groups or individuals more than once. The details surrounding the experiences or conditions are different in each case; there are, in fact, only eight explicit references and therefore the interpretation put upon them, the deductions drawn from them have to be put into the context of the much fuller and wider teaching concerning the person and work of the Holy Spirit found elsewhere in the Gospels and in the Epistles.

The references to groups of Christians are found in Acts 2:4 where, on the day of Pentecost, we read, "And they were all filled with the Holy Ghost, and began to speak with other tongues." Many scholars would ask us to treat what happened on the day of Pentecost as a unique happening and therefore we cannot make any deductions from it without a very real degree of caution. For example, the tongues referred to here would seem to have no connection whatsoever with the speaking in tongues set forth as a gift of the Spirit later on in Scripture and recorded elsewhere. In the Pentecost experience there was no interpretation and the reaction described in verse 8 is of everyone hearing in his own language the wonderful works of God. This is something quite different from the ecstatic utterances which seemed to characterize the gift of tongues referred to elsewhere in the New Testament. Again in Acts 4:31 we find a similar group, maybe many if not most would be the same people, and here we read they were "filled" again. This time there is no record of any tongues being spoken but instead they "spake the word of God with boldness." It would seem as if the need to be "filled" had arisen again. Is it possible that the blessing had been lost, and if so that it had to be renewed?

There are several references to individual Christians either being "filled" or being "full" of the Holy Ghost and these are more frequent. It is recorded of Peter, in Acts 4:8 when he appeared before the authorities, we read, "Then Peter, filled with the Holy Ghost, said . . ." No doubt Peter had also been in both the other groups concerned, so it would seem as if on three occasions he was filled with the Holy Ghost. It is recorded of Paul in Acts 9:17 when Ananias went into him, blinded as he had been by the light that had shone round him on the road to Damascus. Ananias declared that part at least of the purpose of God was "that thou mightest . . . be filled with the Holy Ghost." In this context it was something obviously in the intention of God for St. Paul from the very moment of his conversion. Again in Acts 13:9 when we read of Paul at Paphos in Cyprus, when he was opposed by Elymas, the sorcerer, we are told that "Paul, filled with the Holy Ghost, set his eyes on him" and then passed the divine judgment of blindness upon him. It is also written of other individuals: the seven deacons appointed to look after the social obligations of the church in Jerusalem were all to be men "full of the Spirit and of wisdom" (Acts 6:3—RSV). It is recorded of Stephen in verse 5 of that same chapter that he was "a man full of faith and of the Holy Ghost." It is also recorded of Barnabas in Acts 11:24 that he was "a good man and full of the Holy Ghost."

So this "being filled" with the Spirit or being "full" of the Spirit is recorded both of groups and also of individuals. It is also recorded both as a specific experience which apparently could be and was repeated, and also as a condition which was recognized by other Christians that a man was "full" of the Holy Ghost.

We can therefore note in our study of this particular aspect of the person and work of the Holy Spirit that it is *recorded of* Christians, We also want to note that it is:

2. *Required of Christians.* "Be not drunk with wine, wherein is excess; but be filled with the Spirit," Paul wrote in Ephesians 5:18. It is worth noting two things here:

(a) that the obligation to be filled with the Spirit is laid upon *every Christian*. This being "filled with the

29

Spirit" is what God required, not just of ministers, or workers, or apostles, or missionaries; it is set within the context in which Paul goes on to speak of husbands and wives, of children and parents, of servants and masters. "Be filled with the Holy Spirit" is not simply something for preaching but for *living*. It is also worth noting:

(b) that the duration is for *every moment*. The tense here is the present tense. What Paul is saying is "Be ye continually being filled with the Spirit." Dr. Paul Rees has a helpful distinction that he makes between what he calls a *crucial* and a *continual* being filled with the Spirit. Here then is a condition to be maintained—Paul is not referring to an experience of a moment but the experience of a lifetime. With this variety and these different references, although there are not so very many of them, we have to try and probe behind the differences and the record, and see what deductions we can make; we must find out if there are any guiding lines or principles to determine what all this is intended to mean to us.

I want to stress three conclusions that I have drawn. The first is that being filled, or being full of the Holy Ghost, seems to me to suggest:

A. *An assent that being filled with the Spirit presumes.* This word "filled" is a word of degree. It suggests the possibility of the *presence* of the Holy Spirit without being *filled* with the Holy Spirit. The very fact that there is a command to "be filled" carries with it the implication that it is possible not to be filled. But when we consider that the word "filled" is a word of degree and that the word is related to a person, we face the fact again that you cannot have more or less of a person. You can, however, have more or less of a person's trust. You can allow a person more or less liberty or freedom in your home.

Sister Eva of Friedenshort speaks of this in a vivid phrase where she describes the presence of the Holy Spirit in the lives of some Christians as being like that of a "prisoner without power." I believe that if the *baptism* of the Spirit is the terminology used to describe a *receiving* of the person of the Spirit, then that of being *filled* with the Spirit is the terminology used to describe a *releasing* of the Holy Spirit in our lives. And what does this involve?

(i) *An assent to the activity of the Holy Spirit* in our lives—a willingness. It begins with an attitude of total willingness for the Holy Spirit to do in me what He wants to do and what He has been sent to do. There will be no restriction imposed on His activity; there will be no restraining hand stretched out by me. So many of us treat the Holy Spirit like we treat the dentist, especially if the dentist is a new one and we are not sure if he knows how far he can go before we squeal! In that case our hand is never far away from his hand so that we can stop him doing what he wants to do whenever it begins to hurt.

In order to be filled crucially and in order to be filled continually, there must be then this utter willingness, this complete readiness for anything and for everything. Sometimes our reservations will vary: we may restrict the amount of the activities of the Holy Spirit; we may restrict the nature of the activities of the Holy Spirit. But how essential it is for every Christian to find out what the activities, what the ministries of the Holy Spirit are meant to be—not His gifts—and then to allow Him to do them. He has been given to teach, therefore we must give Him the opportunities to teach us. He has been given to lead, then we must be willing to obey when

31

His leading comes. He has been given to pray, then we must allow Him to pray, in us and through us. He has been given to testify of Christ, therefore we must be willing to open our mouths. He has been given to glorify Christ, then our motives must be utterly unselfish and pure. He has been given to live the kind of life now that God would have us live hereafter. He is called "the earnest", that is, a pre-sample of what is to come. He has been given to seal our lives as belonging to God, therefore we must recognize the ownership of God over every part of our lives. The urge, the promptings will come. The significant part that we play is how we respond to these urgings and these promptings. Those who were filled, were filled because they were ready and willing to be filled.

(ii) *An assent to the authority of the Holy Spirit.* He comes not just to do but He comes to be. And this involves a willingness to put out of our lives anything that is inconsistent with His character and to bring into our lives anything that is consistent with His character, and His character is revealed by His names. He is the Spirit of Love: the Spirit of Truth: the Spirit of Holiness: the Spirit of Christ: the Spirit of God. He not only wants to *do* so much in me and through me, He also wants to *be* so much in me, to me and through me. And where this assent is lacking then the Holy Spirit is grieved. Ephesians 4:30 tells us "grieve not the Spirit." How do we grieve the Holy Spirit? Surely we grieve Him when we fail to allow Him to do in us that for which He has been given; when we fail to allow Him to be in us that which He wants to be.

The second deduction I make concerns:

B. *The attack that being filled with the Spirit provokes.* I find that the context here has two basic elements, both of them breathe an atmosphere of turbulence. Being filled with the Spirit is associated with:

(i) *Equipment for witness.* On the day of Pentecost they were no sooner filled than they were on their feet, their tongues were loosed and they were speaking. In Acts 2:4 we read, "they ... began to speak," in verse 14—"Peter standing up with the eleven, lifted up his voice, and said"; Acts 4:8 "Then Peter, filled ... said"; Acts 4:31 "they were all filled ... and they spake the word of God with boldness." In chapter 9:20 Paul "straightway ... preached Christ"; Acts 13:9 "Saul ... filled ... said." Equipment for witness.

But even here care is needed. Some people are in danger of assuming that whenever they are filled with the Spirit this will result in tremendous blessing, that thousands will be converted to faith in Christ as happened in Jerusalem on the day of Pentecost and later, as well as in Samaria. But the records of big movements of this nature are confined to these occasions. Was Paul not filled with the Spirit when he went to Athens? And how many responded there? Was Paul not filled with the Spirit when he went to Corinth? And how many were converted there? Surely Paul was continually being filled with the Spirit, and yet in the greater part of his missionary journeys the response was small! The reason for the exceptional responses in Jerusalem and the response in Samaria was, surely, that these were fields where the seed had been well sown and well tended by the ministry of Christ, and there was a great harvest to reap. Equipment for witness? Yes, when we are filled with the Spirit we speak.

(ii) *Engagement in warfare.* Being filled with the Spirit

always builds up a swift reaction, a negative reaction of ridicule and mockery (Acts 2:13) or a negative reaction of resistance and threats (Acts 4:21). But there can be a positive reaction, too—the Holy Spirit convicting men of sin, the sin of not believing in Christ, then being brought to faith in Him and into the fellowship, the unity to be found in Him. But let us remember that being filled with the Spirit is not an experience that leads into a peaceful, easy, comfortable Christian experience but rather into one of turbulence and battle.

Then finally we can note:

C. *The answer that being filled with the Spirit provides.* There are two basic problems that call for an answer in the life of the Church. The first is:

(i) *An indifference towards the Church* seen in a disregard of the Church and its message as being out of date, irrelevant, being dull and drab. One thing that could safely be said about the Christians in the days of the early Church was that they could never be ignored. Someone once said that wherever Paul went there was either a riot or a revival. That was simply because the pattern of life lived by the Christian was a condemnation of the whole pattern of life lived by society. In the life of a Christian there was also a transformation produced by the power of the Spirit of God releasing the life of the risen Lord that demonstrated a totally different and a much better way of life. This was so dramatic and the contrast so striking that the Christian could never be ignored. How desperately we need this kind of impact today and it will only come when Christians are "being filled with the Spirit of God." The other problem is that of:

(ii) *An incompetence within the Church.* Incompetence

34

and impotence! But these Christians filled with the Spirit we find were instructed Christians. What an amazing grasp of truth they seemed to get so quickly. They seemed to be inspired with a new motivation—that of love. They were concerned about the work of their Lord, concerned for His glory and for His kingdom. It grieved them that so many people ignored Him and were indifferent to His claims. But not only were they concerned for the worth of their Lord, they recognized the worth of their fellows and they were driven to their knees in prayer; they were set upon their feet in witness. Far from being incompetent they were able, instructed, sure of their message, confident in their Lord, willing to challenge society, willing to speak up, to go to jail if need be.

What do we know of all this today? There is, possibly, no need so urgent as the need for every Christian to find out what it means to be filled with the Spirit, for every one of us to be in a condition of being filled continually with the Spirit, of allowing the Holy Spirit to be in us what He wants to be and to do in us what He wants to do. It was recorded then! Is it recorded of us now? It was required then! Surely it is required of us now! And so you and I face the challenge of obedience to this command, "Be ye continually being filled with the Spirit." And we face the question as we face the command—are we willing to allow Him to do in us what He wants to do? Amen Are we willing to allow Him to be in us what He wants to be? That way, and that way alone will bring us into the experience, crucial it may be but then continual, of "being filled with the Spirit."

When I was a boy, one of the things we loved to do in our holidays in the Scottish Highlands was to dam up a small burn. We would fill the bed of the stream with

35

big rocks; we would fill the crannies and gaps in the rocks with turf hacked off the banks and gradually a great pool of water would build up behind. The bed of the burn below the dam was dry, the bed above was full. It was fun to build the dam and watch the pool grow but then there came the final climax of delight when we broke the dam down and through the gap the pent-up waters surged—released.

At the baptism of the Spirit which came to us at our conversion, we received the person of the Spirit; being filled with the Spirit is different. Here it is not a matter of receiving, it is a matter of releasing the Spirit so that He may have His way in our lives, anytime! anywhere! in anything!

5 The Fruit of the Spirit

JOHN 15:1–10. GALATIANS 5:22, 23

We are now to consider the ultimate object of all that we have so far learned. What is the goal towards which the person and work of the Holy Spirit is moving? What is He aiming at? What is the one thing that we should be concerned about? What is the one thing that we should be looking for?

This is where I find Christians, in my judgment, nine times out of ten go completely wrong. The final evidence of being filled with the Spirit of God is that the fruit of the Spirit is seen in our lives, and the fruit of the Spirit is character! I have never yet heard Christians pray that their lives may be evidently bearing the fruit of the Spirit. Never! I have heard them praying for gifts. I have heard them praying that they might be filled with the Spirit. But none seem to have their eyes on the objective, the final objective, the crowning evidence in their lives that they are being filled with the Spirit. This crowning evidence in anybody's life is not whether they possess this gift or that gift; it is not whether they have had this experience or that experience. The final evidence that a life is being filled with the Spirit is when, in that life, *Amen* there can be seen the fruit of the Spirit. This is the goal; this is the climax; this is the crowning evidence. And I have found to my dismay that some Christians who claim certain experiences, who lay great stress on certain gifts, seem to break down totally here. There is no evidence—

37

or little enough—that in their lives there is being seen the fruit of the Spirit.

I used to think that the fruit of the Spirit was orthodoxy —lots of evangelicals used to take that line—and then I woke up with a sense of shock one day when I realized that the fruit of the Spirit is character. It is the kind of person you are or, if you like to be more precise, how Christ-like you are. "The fruit of the Spirit is love." Some people would stop there and say that what follows is an amplification of love. Others would say love is the first of this nine-fold cluster of fruit. I really like to think that you make a pause there and that what follows are simply manifestations of love: "joy, peace, long-suffering, gentleness, goodness, faithfulness, meekness, temperance (or self control): against such there is no law."

I want to sketch out in outline what, it seems to me, we need to hold in balance when we are thinking in terms of the fruit of the Spirit. First there is something basic on which I think everyone reading this would agree, although it is just possible there might be somebody who needs to get this emphasis—somebody who isn't a Christian at all. You are just a Church person but not a Christian; you've never been born again of the Spirit, never received the Spirit. Let's begin just where you are and get a hold of this fact: when we are thinking in terms of the fruit of the Spirit we face what I have called:

A. *The necessity of a Presence.* To talk of "the fruit of the Spirit" means, surely, that there cannot be fruit unless there is life! That is self evident. So there is:

(i) *An assumption that we dare not make.* The assumption that a lot of church folk make—and I am afraid a lot of ministers who ought to know a lot better make it, too—is that everybody in the church has already received the gift of the Holy Spirit, that they have already been born again. This is not what Scripture teaches. Romans 8:9 states quite clearly the possibility of a man not having the Holy Spirit: "if any man have not the Spirit of Christ, he is none of His." Acts 19:2 is a verse often completely misquoted and misapplied, when Paul is speaking to that little group at Ephesus whose instruction was incomplete—the teaching they had received was based upon the expectations aroused by John the Baptist concerning Christ, but not upon an experience of the new birth. Paul's question was not, "Have ye received the Holy Ghost since ye believed?" but "Did you receive the Holy Spirit when you believed?" (RSV). And they replied, "No, we have never even heard that there is a Holy Spirit" (RSV). Never heard of Him! Well, obviously these people were religious but not regenerate! So it is possible to be a member of the Church without being a member of Christ and without having understood enough to have received the Holy Spirit. That kind of a person is really in an absurd situation. They are expecting the fruit of the Spirit and they don't possess the life of the Spirit. And that is just ridiculous. They are trying to live the Christian life and they haven't got it! Well, that is stupid! God doesn't ask you to live the Christian life until you have it, or rather until you have Him. So, if there is an assumption that we dare not make, there is:

(ii) *An acceptance we must not delay*. If we are not sure then let's make sure. Well, you say, how do we receive the Holy Spirit? Simply as God's gift. In Acts 2:38 it is crystal clear: "repent ... receive." In other words, "receive as a gift the new life, which God offers you through Christ, of the indwelling Spirit." That means

39

quite simply we don't earn, we don't deserve, we cannot buy, we can simply receive as a gift this new life. "The gift of God is eternal life"; "God so loved the world, that He gave." It is a giving by God and a receiving by us. When do we receive the Holy Spirit? The moment we put our faith into Christ. In Ephesians 1:13, Paul writes of Christ "in whom also after that ye believed, ye were sealed with that Holy Spirit of promise." You believed —you received. Believing is your part, bestowing is God's part. We repent—God responds. God's response to faith put into Christ is to put His Spirit into us.

Next we have to face:

B. *The mystery of a process.* Whether in the realm of nature or of grace, when we consider the growth of a plant, the forming of a flower, the perfecting of the fruit; the growth of a soul, the transformation of a life, two factors emerge. First there are:

(i) *Ways that we may not understand.* Take what flower you will, there is an element of mystery and miracle clean beyond the wit of man to reproduce. How does the rose come to be the rose? Why is it that there is that exquisite colour, that amazing fragrance, that perfect shape? What controls the processes which transform what the plant draws from the soil and the air, from the sun and the rain into that exquisite flower? What processes are involved? We just don't know.

There is a lovely verse in Deuteronomy 29:29: "The secret things belong unto the Lord our God: but those things which are revealed belong unto us and to our children for ever." I have never forgotten hearing Dr. Sangster preach on that text at Filey, and I remember that he said, "There are some things we do not know." Then he added—and this is a lovely phrase—"There is a

reverent agnosticism that goes hand in hand with faith."
Now the word agnosticism means simply "not knowing."
There are some things we do not know: there is a reverent
agnosticism that goes hand in hand with faith. "The
secret things belong unto the Lord our God." In other
words, God doesn't explain everything.

If that is so in the realm of nature, so it is in the realm
of grace. There are things beyond my understanding but
they happen before my eyes. The life that knows the
incoming of the life of the Spirit of God becomes
mysteriously and miraculously a different life. A girl
that found the Bible the most boring book in the world
so that she could never be bothered to read it suddenly
finds it has become the most fascinating book in the
world and she cannot stop reading it. How do you explain
that? There are ways we may not understand but there is:

(ii) *Work we must not underrate.* That field clothed with
golden corn; those trees in that orchard laden with fruit;
that galaxy of colour and fragrance in our garden; there
is an element of mystery about it all but there is an element of drudgery too. All that abundance of fruit is no
accident. It is the result of man's co-operation with the
laws of nature, and when we co-operate with the laws
of the spiritual world it will involve a similar drudgery,
a similar discipline, but it will produce a similar delight.
There is no short cut to spiritual fulness and fruit. I don't
know of any experience in the Bible that can take place
in a given moment of time which promises a solution
to all my problems from that moment on and leaves me
in a kind of dreamy daze where everything is beautiful.
That man whose Christian life is so outstanding may
find there is much in his life that he doesn't understand
but there is much more that he does. You will find there

is a daily discipline, there is a spiritual drudgery that ensures that the Holy Spirit is allowed to do and be in that man's life what he wants to do and be.

Spiritual growth demands understanding. It is never fostered by ignorance. You will find that kind of man on his knees; you will find that he knows all about obedience to the will of God and what that means; you will find that man in the company of other Christians learning from them and learning with them. If you come across a beautiful garden you will know that somebody has been working in it. If you pass a farm and there is a wonderful harvest you know that somebody has been sweating there. The mystery of a process—much that we do not understand, much that we must not underrate. And then we come to the climax of it all:

C. *The quality of a product.* "The fruit of the Spirit is love, joy, peace, longsuffering, gentleness, goodness, faithfulness, meekness, self control" (Gal. 5:22, 23). That is to say, the objective that God is working at and towards is character that is Christ-like. I want us to note first what I have called:

(i) *The perfection of it.* Love—that is the opposite of selfishness. Mary Slessor jotted down in her Bible: "Love = live for." Here was a life in which there was a motivation that compelled service of others. Love is unceasingly active on behalf of others. It is a motivation that compels service and an appreciation that directs service. If it is a true love it is marked by a rare and wise insight; there is nothing irrelevant or blundering about what it does. I think it is Dr. Scroggie in his tremendous book on *The Love Life*, who talks about clumsy piety, blundering goodness the kind of people who would think they are doing the right thing but they would be doing it in the wrong way. There is a classic illustration that comes from my experience. A lady worshipping in Charlotte Chapel to whom God had spoken through His Word remained bowed in prayer, a Christian of mature years. Another blundering and clumsy ham-handed Christian came up to her to ask her if she was saved. Now the Holy Spirit didn't tell that Christian to do that; the Holy Spirit knew the lady was saved, had been saved for years, but some great "thick" of a Christian in whose life the Holy Spirit certainly was not having His way came blundering. Love has utter unselfishness and an incredibly tender insight.

Joy! Are we really joyful? I often think of L. F. E. Wilkinson—some of you have never heard of him. If ever a man had a beaming face Wilkie had. He was always called "Wilkie" or L.F.E. His face just shone. It was as if the sun had suddenly come through when he went on to the platform. He had an irrepressible sense of humour and when he got up to speak at Keswick it seemed as if a ray of sunshine just went over the whole tent and everybody beamed back at him. Joy! Some of us have faces as long as Leith Walk. (If you don't know how long Leith Walk is, go and tread it!) Beaming countenance, elastic step, the singing voice which is independent of circumstances that always change, because its source is in the Lord. "Rejoice in the Lord", said Paul. You remember Billy Bray. Folk got tired of his "Hallelujahs" and his "Praise the Lord" which came bubbling up effervescently all the time until somebody said, "Billy Bray, what somebody needs to do to you is to take you and put you in a barrel with the lid on, and shut you down and shut you up. What would you do then?" To which Billy replied, "I'd look for the bung-hole and shout 'Glory' through it." Quite irrepressible! Independent of circumstances and evident to onlookers is an inner joy that shows.

Peace! Not an escape from but a knowing the answer to. Peace, that possession of adequate resources that looks at the facts then views them through Christ and finds in Him an adequacy to cope with any situation. A class of children were once asked to draw a picture of peace and one child drew a thundering waterfall and just by its edge a mother bird on its nest, sitting there right alongside the thunder.

Longsuffering! A patient endurance, an ability to endure, to hold on, to put up with the weaknesses we encounter in others and the irritation that starts tempers rising and tongues wagging, the ability to endure in the work we endeavour for God. So many Christians start and then leave it undone. "Ye did run well; who did hinder you?" (Galatians 5:7). It is sometimes said in commendation of a person that he doesn't suffer fools gladly. All I can say is that if that's the kind of person we are, we're certainly not bearing the fruit of the Spirit.

Gentleness! In speech or in touch. Sensitive to the feelings of others. Not willing to cause unnecessary hurt or needless injury. The gentleness of a doctor's or a surgeon's hand: gentleness yet firmness. Courtesy, consideration. I love that story of Prince Edward when he was Prince of Wales, in India. He was at a banquet and many Indian princes were there and they were not quite familiar with the etiquette of the Western world. Part of the furnishings on the table was the provision of finger bowls, a bowl filled with scented water so that when you have eaten fruit or handled something greasy you can dip your fingers in it, wash them and dry them on your napkin or serviette. This Indian prince did not know what the bowl was and he thought he should drink the water so he drank it. Before any other person could smile or even raise an eyebrow, and before there could be the faintest ripple of comment, the Prince of Wales immediately took his finger bowl and drank the contents too, because nobody would dare laugh at him. So the Indian prince was covered.

Goodness! Sheer downright goodness in a world gone foul. Good all through: good all the time. Not out of the world but in the world. There are some Christians who think we have to withdraw from all physical contact with worldly people. Our Lord's life was lived continually in contact with the worst. The miracle of His life was that He lived it without sin, without compromise. He didn't deviate one iota from what He knew to be pleasing to the Father. He was right alongside it, He was rubbing shoulders with it. They condemned Him. They said, "This man eats with publicans and sinners." He has harlots at His board. He did, but His goodness was such that it wasn't infected, it wasn't corrupted.

Faithfulness! A dependability that never gives up and never lets down. Can you imagine Jesus Christ ever letting anybody down? How many Christians do you know who do precisely that? They let people down. They let the minister down. They let the members of the congregation down. They take over a church magazine district and don't do it. They take up a Sunday-school class and half the time they are never there. They join the choir but they only come occasionally, if they have nothing else to do. Faithfulness! Reliability! Dependability! Jesus was utterly dependable. This is part of the fruit of the Spirit.

Meekness! When I tried to get a definition of meekness this phrase came to me and I believe it is true. Meekness is that attitude of mind that can receive injury without resentment and praise without pride. Meekness. Humility. There is a story of the great Dr. Whyte of Free St. George's. A man went to see Dr. Whyte, one of the greatest preachers that Scotland has ever known, and reported on having met somebody who had voiced the opinion that Dr. Hood Wilson of the Barclay Church was unconverted. Dr. Whyte was angry. He got up and strode up and down his study, saying to himself over and over again "the rascal." Then the visitor went on, "But, Dr. Whyte, this man I was talking to said something worse than that. He said you weren't converted." Dr. Whyte stood still. Then he went to his desk and he said to this stranger, "Please leave me" and he put his head down on his hands on his desk before God to search his soul. Humility. Meekness that receives injury without resentment and praise without pride. You know why some of us never really experience any of the true filling of the Spirit of God? Because we couldn't stand it. We would become insufferably conceited. And God sometimes has to take some of us through the most terrible disciplines of suffering so that every motivation that might have the least thought of pride or self-conceit is absolutely smashed to smithereens. Meekness.

Self-control! The stability of life based upon a rigid discipline that pursues its chosen career undisturbed and undistracted.

This is the perfection of fruit and there is:

(ii) *The attraction of it.* We have all seen a garden that is a mass of colour, beauty and order. We have maybe walked down a lane and seen a bramble bush laden with fruit; we have passed an orchard and seen the boughs bending low under the weight of the fruit; we have seen a field of golden corn and found it attractive and arresting. I want to submit to you that when you and I are being continually filled with the Spirit of God, and the fruit of the Spirit with drudgery and discipline is being produced in our lives and characters, we will be living a quality of life that just cannot be ignored—a quality of life that can be explained only in terms of deity.

The fruit of the Spirit is character. The ultimate goal towards which all that the Holy Spirit is, and all that the Holy Spirit gives, and all that the Holy Spirit does in your life and mine—the ultimate goal of all that is what? It is simply so that you and I become like Christ. That's all! And that's enough isn't it?

To be Filled w/ the Spirit is to be Born of the Spirit.

6 The Significance of the Symbolism of Scripture

JOHN 3:1–17

We are all familiar with the fact that in Scripture truths are very often illuminated with meaning and insight by the use of illustrations. These may take the form of parables or miracles, the latter being so often simply parables in action, or they may be by the use of some analogy or metaphor, some illustration taken from ordinary life which serves to illumine the truths in the spiritual realm.

When we turn to this aspect of the teaching of Scripture concerning the person and work of the Holy Spirit in the life of the believer, we find that in the Word of God there are four very familiar things from everyday life that are used to throw additional light upon the ministry of the Holy Spirit. In the first place we find light thrown upon what I would call:

A. *The sanctifying work of the Holy Spirit* by the use, in John 3, of a reference to the symbol of the Holy Spirit as being like the wind. Verse 8 of that chapter reads: "The wind bloweth where it listeth, and thou hearest the sound thereof, but canst not tell whence it cometh, and whither it goeth: so is every one that is born of the Spirit." I realize that primarily this reference to the Holy Spirit's activity being like the wind refers to the new birth and it is, of course, in connection with the operation of the Holy Spirit in regeneration or, if you prefer, in conversion that this analogy is used. And it is worth noting, too, that this was one aspect of the conversion experience of the disciples on the day of Pentecost when we read in Acts 2:2: "And suddenly a sound came from heaven like the rush of a mighty wind, and it filled all the house where they were sitting" (RSV).

It is this life-giving, transforming operation of the Holy Spirit that is also envisaged in the vision of the valley full of dry bones given to Ezekiel in the Old Testament and recorded in Ezekiel 37:1–14, where the word "wind" and "breath" in the Hebrew are the same. And the promise with which that account of the vision of the prophet ends is with the Lord saying in verse 14 that He will "put my Spirit in you, and ye shall live."

To turn back to the words of our Lord to Nicodemus we can make two deductions from what is recorded. We see that it is:

(i) *The Spirit who gives life.* Just as the wind is ceaselessly active, just as the wind is always blowing and we hear the sound of it, so the Holy Spirit is ceaselessly, restlessly on the move seeking an entrance into hearts and lives so that they may be regenerated and renewed. Sometimes the wind may blow more strongly, sometimes more gently; sometimes the wind blows with seemingly irresistible force, sometimes with scarcely discernible movement. You recall how this is expressed in that loveliest of all hymns about the Holy Spirit which begins with the words: "Our blest Redeemer, ere He breathed." In verse 3 the hymn-writer puts it thus: "He came in tongues of living flame, to teach, convince, subdue; all powerful as the wind He came, as viewless too."

How many of us have memories of great crusades, like the Billy Graham Crusades at Harringay, Earls Court or in the Kelvin Hall, when the wind of the Spirit has been blowing almost at gale force and the hearts and wills of men and women have been bending over like trees bending before the storm? At other times there has been a total absence of turbulence, either of oratory or emotion, but a stillness that could be felt and in that stillness that gentle voice was heard "soft as the breath of even."

Yes, the Spirit gives life, new life, the very life of Christ and men are born again, and because He is the Holy Spirit this is what makes it possible for men to live a holy life. That is why I have called this symbol one illustrating the sanctifying work of the Holy Spirit; that is in the fullest possible sense of the word "sanctify"—a word which suggests not simply the coming of a new life but the making of a new man. But there is something more; we can see here not only that it is the Spirit who gives life but also that it is:

(ii) *The Spirit who is Lord.* "The wind blows where it wills," said our Lord "and you hear the sound of it, but you do not know whence it comes or whither it goes; so it is with every one who is born of the Spirit" (RSV). Not only in the experience of conversion but also in the area of Christian experience we must accept the sovereignty of the Spirit. So many of us want to contain the Holy Spirit, to confine Him, to control Him and thus to control the lives He would seek to enter and change, to bless and use. We have a formula for Revival; we have a predetermined plan for Evangelism; we have set ideas about this or that, and unless others agree and accept what we have to say then we brush them aside. Then to our utter amazement and complete confusion the Holy Spirit comes as a wind and blows our whole preconceived ideas out of the window.

I remember so clearly that when I first came to St.

George's-Tron I was criticized by some because I did not preach what they chose to call "the Gospel" every Sunday night but I can think of at least two lives which found Christ through messages that were really preached and addressed to Christians. We need to remember that the whole of the Word of God is the "sword of the Spirit." I love that phrase: "You do not know whence the wind comes or *whither* it goes." Here the Spirit is Lord. We cannot tell what issues may arise out of the yielding to the power of the Spirit of God; only He the Holy Spirit knows. Little did I know when, as a schoolboy, I accepted Christ where the wind of the Spirit would blow me and take me literally all over the world. So here we have the wind as the symbol of the regenerating, renewing work of the Holy Spirit—His sanctifying ministry.

There is another symbol used in the Word of God which throws light upon what I am calling:

B. *The qualifying work of the Holy Spirit.* This is the symbol of oil which in the New Testament is identified with what we call "the anointing of the Spirit." In the Old Testament the anointing with oil was for the service of God, either a service rendered by a priest or a king and he was always anointed with oil. Not only were people anointed with oil but furnishings in the Tabernacle were similarly anointed, setting them apart for the service of God. In the New Testament the symbol disappears and is replaced in the thinking and experience of Christians by that which was symbolized, namely, the person and work of the Holy Spirit.

In this connection I feel we must strike a note of warning about this aspect of the person and work of the Holy Spirit. While in the Old Testament the Scriptures speak frequently of this anointing with oil of people and of

51

things to be used in the service or worship of God, in the New Testament the references are few. There are two or three references to our Lord being anointed by the Spirit. In Luke 4:18, in His visit to Nazareth, our Lord applies to Himself the words of the prophet Isaiah: "the Lord ... hath anointed me to preach the gospel." In Acts 4:27 Peter refers to "Jesus, whom thou hast anointed" and in Acts 10:38 in the house of Cornelius Peter again refers to our Lord saying, "How God anointed Jesus of Nazareth with the Holy Ghost and with power." In all these references the context would seem to be that of an anointing for service and, in all probability, refers to what happened at our Lord's baptism when the Holy Spirit, we are told, descended upon Him as a dove. Dr. Campbell Morgan points out that we are not necessarily justified in applying all the experiences in the life of our Lord to our own experience. To that cautionary statement, however, this reply can be made, that by virtue of our union with Christ by the Holy Spirit surely we have been united with Him not simply in His death and resurrection but also with Him in His baptism and what happened there. It was at the baptism of our Lord, when He identified Himself in baptism with the need of the world, that He was anointed by the Holy Spirit.

The references to an anointing referring to Christians are only two and both would appear to refer to one special aspect of the conversion experience of the believer, something in which every believer shares. The two references are (1) in 2 Corinthians 1:21 and 22 where St. Paul writes, "Now he which stablisheth us with you in Christ, and hath anointed us, is God; Who hath also sealed us, and given the earnest of the Spirit in our hearts." Here the anointing would appear to be something in which all had shared at their conversion, just as the sealing and the earnest of the Spirit refers to what happened at our conversion. The word translated by "anointed" in the AV is translated "commissioned" in the RSV and this is maybe giving the significance of the anointing—commissioned for service. Another reference to this anointing referring specifically to Christians is found (2) in 1 John 2:27 where John writes, "But the anointing which you received from him abides in you, and you have no need that anyone should teach you; as his anointing teaches you about everything, and is true, and is no lie, just as it has taught you, abide in him" (RSV). Here the anointing is related to our understanding of the mind, the truth, the Word of God. What can we deduce then from all these references? I think there are two things at least. The anointing of the Spirit in which every believer has participated is related to:

(i) *The tasks we must undertake in the service of God.* It refers to that part of the ministry of the Holy Spirit which in the first place makes us aware of what that task is and in the second place makes us able for what that task demands. In other words, when you and I were saved we were saved for something. The anointing of the Spirit is for service. The Holy Spirit will make me aware of what that particular task is for me in the whole over-all purpose of God and will also make me able for it. In this sense, at my conversion I was not only regenerated by the Holy Spirit but I was separated by the Holy Spirit for service. In Psalm 92:10 there is a lovely sentence where the Psalmist exclaims, "I shall be anointed with fresh oil," and I like to think that every time I face a fresh task in the will of God there is available a fresh anointing of the Spirit of

God. The second thing we can deduce from these references to the anointing or the unction of the Holy Spirit in which every believer shares has reference to:

(ii) *The truths we must understand in the service of God.* These are truths contained in the Word of God, the truths concerned with the ways of God, and this anointing of the Holy Spirit gives us the insights that we need. Basically speaking, then, while there is a special ministry of teaching, a special gift of the Holy Spirit for teaching, there is another sense in which every Christian has his own Teacher in the indwelling Holy Spirit, who by His anointing and unction gives us spiritual insight. This is, of course, something absolutely true. So the sanctifying work of the Holy Spirit is illustrated by the reference to "the wind"; the qualifying work of the Holy Spirit is illustrated by reference to "the oil." Thirdly, we find in Scripture a symbol which throws light upon what I have called:

C. *The satisfying work of the Holy Spirit,* and here the reference is to water. There are two clear references to this in John's gospel. In John 4:13 and 14 Christ speaks to the thirsting soul of the woman by the well at Sychar saying, "Whosoever drinketh of this water shall thirst again: but whosoever drinketh of the water that I shall give him shall never thirst; but the water that I shall give him shall be in him a well of water springing up into everlasting life." The other reference is also in John and is also familiar. "If any one thirst, let him come to me and drink. He who believes in me . . . out of his heart shall flow rivers of living water. Now this he said about the Spirit" (John 7:37–39 RSV). The Old Testament prophets had spoken in similar vein; in Isaiah 44:3 we read of the promise of God: "I will pour water upon him that is thirsty, and floods upon the dry ground: I will pour my spirit upon thy seed, and my blessing upon thine offspring." There are two pictures here: the first is that of:

(i) *The welling up of the water within.* There is a satisfaction that is only found when the cleansing, renewing, life-giving ministry of the grace and the Spirit of God is being exercised in the soul. All these references are to thirst and the quenching of that thirst, and this is what suggests the title for this aspect as being the satisfying ministry and work of the Holy Spirit. But there is also:

(ii) *The spilling over of the water without.* Here is a spring within of fresh water welling up and spilling over so that rivers of living water reaching other lives bring to them, too, the offer of a similar renewing experience, a similar satisfaction; bringing freshness, fruitfulness, loveliness, to lives that have known only dryness and barrenness. How incredible the transformation can be when the water comes. Those who know the Middle East, the lands where there is a shortage of water and rain, know what a tremendous transformation there is almost overnight when the monsoon comes and the land is drenched with water. In Ezekiel 47 there is a wonderful picture of an ever deepening river and the final comment in verse 9 is that, "it shall come to pass, that every thing that liveth, which moveth, whithersoever the rivers shall come, shall live." I always remember hearing, I think it was, Lindsay Glegg saying that he remembered hearing a girl saying in a prayer, "Lord, I can't hold much but I can overflow lots." And Mr. Lindsay Glegg added, "and the overflow would hide the vessel."

The final symbol that I find in the Word of God to which I want to refer is the symbol of:

D. *The purifying work of the Holy Spirit* and this is, of

55

course, the symbol of fire. We have already referred in an earlier study to the promise and prophecy of John the Baptist concerning the ministry of our Lord: "He shall baptize you with the Holy Ghost and with fire." And so it was that on the day of Pentecost, we read in Acts 2:3, "There appeared to them tongues as of fire, distributed and resting on each one of them" (RSV). Fire is frequently found in the Bible as symbolizing the holiness of God. In Hebrews 12:29, "our God is a consuming fire"; in Revelation 4:5 we read that "there were seven lamps of fire burning before the throne, which are the seven Spirits of God"—not that there are seven Holy Spirits but the number seven in Scripture is used in the sense of completeness or perfection. In Isaiah 4:4 we read of the Spirit of God as "the spirit of burning." In the challenge of Elijah the basis of that challenge was "the God that answereth by fire, let him be God" . . . and so we could go on. I want us to note just two things about what fire does:

(i) *What fire can reveal.* In Malachi 3:3 we read that the Lord "shall sit as a refiner and purifier of silver," and as the metal is held over the fire in a crucible so the hidden impurities will rise to the surface to be skimmed off until the metal is pure. So the ministry of the Holy Spirit will bring to our consciousness things in our lives, in our motives that are inconsistent with the will of God so that they may be removed until the refiner can see reflected in the purified metal the reflection of his own face. Everybody who has become a Christian is aware of this purifying, this convicting, this revealing ministry of the Holy Spirit. I remember so clearly a lady once saying that one of the difficult things about becoming a Christian was that she had developed a peculiarly sensitive conscience.

And of course this is so; this is part of the purifying work of the Spirit of God. But if there is this thought concerning what fire can reveal, there is another aspect of what fire does and we need to consider:

(ii) *How fire can unite.* It unites in our own modern civilization by what we call welding, the fusing together by fire into a unity of two things that were previously separate. The New Testament has much to say about "the one Spirit" about "the unity of the Spirit" because this unity is an evidence of the work of the Holy Spirit and a testimony to His activity and power in our lives. Sin always separates; sin separates man from God and it separates man from man. The separation that has been brought about by sin is, however, overcome by the unifying work of the Holy Spirit, uniting man to God and man to man.

How desperately we need to be aware of this, that separation is always an evidence of the activity of sin. So many people seem to think otherwise. The Holy Spirit will only separate us from sin but never from believers; the Holy Spirit always unites and fuses and welds together into a living, not an inanimate unity those who are born again of the Spirit of God.

We have, therefore, the four symbols: of wind, of oil, of water, of fire, and they speak to us of the fourfold ministry and work of the Holy Spirit in our lives.

7 Speaking in tongues

1 CORINTHIANS 14

To consider one particular gift of the Spirit—namely the gift of speaking in tongues—we turn to Paul's description of it in 1 Corinthians, chapters 12 and 14. I want to divide our study, again, into three sections. First:

A. *The reasons which must prompt us* in our approach to this subject. Apart from the reason that reference is made to this gift of the Spirit at length by St. Paul in 1 Corinthians 14 and that it is named by him as one of the gifts of the Spirit in 1 Corinthians 12, we face a situation in the Church today where we are confronted with two lines of thought in the minds of certain Christians concerning this gift of the Spirit. They demand our careful consideration:

(i) *There is a prominence assigned to this gift* which, in my judgment, calls for correction. There are certain circles in which the stress on this particular aspect of our experience of the Holy Spirit is almost the sole basis for the existence of a separate denomination, or denominations which have taken to themselves the title "Pentecostal." I don't mind in the least anybody claiming that title as long as they do not, at the same time, deny the same right to other Christians who think differently but, in their judgment, equally biblically about the Holy Spirit. To call some Christians or churches Pentecostal and other biblically-based and Christ-honouring churches not Pentecostal seems to me to be taking things too far!

I would hate to think that I was anything less than a Pentecostal Christian, for surely that simply means a Christian living in the experience of what Pentecost signifies. But what was at one time the prerogative of the Pentecostal Churches—the emphasis in their teaching on the gift of speaking with tongues—has in recent years spread well beyond the confines of the Pentecostal denominations; and in the thinking of many Christians this particular gift of the Holy Spirit has gained a like prominence in their thinking and in their teaching.

On every hand this gift of the Spirit is the subject of discussion. To so many the experience of speaking in tongues is either the most desirable or the most commendable of the gifts of the Spirit. If they possess it they feel that this is the final goal of their ambition; if they do not possess it they feel they ought to and indeed in many cases are rebuked by those who realize that they do not. This is the first reason which prompts us to reconsider the whole question of what the Bible has to say about the gift of the Spirit in the speaking in tongues. The second reason lies in:

(ii) *A significance attached to this gift* of the Spirit which, in my judgment, leads to confusion. The significance that has been attached to this particular gift of the Holy Spirit by many, many Christians lies in two ideas which so many of these dear, and I believe misguided, people have and hold. The first is that *every* Christian ought to possess this gift—a claim which we have already seen in our study of 1 Corinthians 12 is completely unscriptural and unbiblical. And the second idea is that a Christian *cannot* be filled with the Spirit without speaking in tongues, which again in the light of what is recorded in Acts and expounded in 1 Corinthians 12 is completely unwarranted and unjustifiable, leading those who do not know their Bibles thoroughly to discouragement, if not to despair. These two stresses lead such Christians to think that because they do not possess this gift they are not filled with the Spirit and therefore they are second-grade Christians! Secondly, we should note:

B. *The records which guide us* in our approach to this subject. And the records—again may I stress it—will be found in the Scriptures of truth. I dare not base divine truth upon human experience; this can be counterfeit, this can be imaginary. The Word of God is the rock upon which we base our faith and our confidence. I want to know what my Bible has to say, not what Christians have to say. When I turn to the Scriptures I find that there are two areas which I must examine. The first centres on what I have called:

(i) *The experiences recorded* in the Word of God— mainly in the book of Acts. These no doubt stem, we assume, from the description given by our Lord in Mark 16:17 of the signs that would follow the testimony of the Apostles. Note that these words were spoken to the eleven (verse 14). Some Christians would suggest that there is no warrant to assume necessarily that the signs would continue beyond the apostolic ministry and that is a perfectly possible and a legitimate deduction to make. Even so, it is worth noting that speaking "with new tongues" was only one of the signs to follow their ministry; "casting out devils" was another. The handling of poisonous snakes and the drinking of poisoned liquids were others—the one to be handled and the other to be drunk without harm, and so far I have never yet met any Christian who is anxious to possess or practice these particular signs! The healing of the sick completed the pattern. This statement in Mark is the source, but in the RSV you will find that this verse falls in the section printed in smaller type which indicates some very real measure of uncertainty as to whether this section was actually part of Mark's gospel or whether it has been included from another source, which of course could equally well be authentic.

When we turn to the book of the Acts we find two things standing out from the records. The first is the *paucity* of references to the "speaking in tongues." We find that there are *only three*. And the second thing which stands out is that all these three references are found within the account of the conversion experiences of those involved; and these make up only a tiny proportion of the many conversion experiences of men and women recorded in Acts where no reference whatsoever is made to this particular aspect of their conversion experience!

The three references are as follows. In Acts 2:4 it is recorded of all those who made up the one hundred and twenty who met in the upper room. But we have to note that this experience has all the appearance of being different, if not unique. The crowd, we are told, heard them speak "every man . . . in his own language" (verse 6). The miracle, then, was either in the speaking or the hearing and the language was another spoken language which needed no interpreter, something that was recognized and understood immediately by those familiar with it. This is something quite different from that dealt with by Paul in 1 Corinthians 14 and let us remember that as far as Acts 2 is concerned this was the unique conversion experience of the one hundred and twenty when they were, for the first time, indwelt by the Spirit of God. The second reference is in Acts 10:44 following, where

61

in the home of Cornelius, in another conversion experience, prior to those involved being baptized with water baptism they received the Holy Ghost and spoke with tongues. This was another occasion in which a small group shared this experience of "speaking with tongues." In Acts 19:1–7, at Ephesus we have the account of a small group of about twelve disciples who, after they had experienced water baptism, received the Holy Spirit after the laying on of hands (to which no reference is made either in Acts 2 or Acts 10), and they too spoke with tongues. This was, again, a conversion experience for this little group of twelve knew nothing about Christ *no* other than what they had learnt through the reports of the preparatory ministry for the coming of Christ carried out by John the Baptist.

What I find significant about these experiences is simply this, that there are far more conversion experiences recorded in Acts in which there is no mention of any speaking with tongues, and that there is not a single reference anywhere in the book of Acts to a post-conversion experience of either individuals or groups speaking in tongues. This seems to me to indicate that both the prominence assigned to this experience and the significance attached to it by certain Christians are totally unjustifiable and unbiblical. Apparently, speaking in tongues as recorded in the book of Acts was neither prominent nor particularly significant. It was, presumably, a sign that our Lord said would follow the ministry of the Apostles and those Christians who believe that these signs ended with the apostolic era point out *ohhh...* that in 1 Corinthians 13:8 Paul does speak of a time when tongues would cease.

So much then for the experiences recorded. Let us

62

hold steadily before us the paucity of the number of these experiences, remembering that one of these was the unique experience on the day of Pentecost, which reduces to two the number of these occasions recorded in Acts.

The second thing that we need to look at within the Scriptures of truth concerns what I have called:

(ii) *The exposition required.* This we find in 1 Corinthians chapters 12, 13 and particularly 14. It is worth noting that this is the particular emphasis in the Corinthian Church which had apparently got out of hand and out of all balance and proportion. This situation had developed in, or maybe had contributed to, a spiritual condition within that church which was far from satisfactory. It was a church that was divided and it was a church that was living a discreditable life, as far as its testimony and witness was concerned.

There are two things to note concerning Paul's attitude to this gift of the Spirit and the first is where Paul places it in *the list he gives* of the gifts of the Spirit of God. There are three lists given in 1 Corinthians 12. In verses 7 to 10 we find a list of such gifts and there this one of speaking with tongues and interpreting tongues comes *last.* Again in verse 28 this gift comes *last,* as it also does in verse 30. I find this difficult to reconcile with the attitude of those who would seem to put it *first.* Paul certainly puts it last and I feel we are wise to follow the mind of Paul, who surely had the mind of Christ.

The second thing is the place Paul puts this gift in *the life he lives,* using his gifts in the service of God. And here we have Paul's evaluation in verses 18 and 19 of chapter 14, where he says, "in the church I had rather speak five words with my understanding, that by my voice I might teach others also, than ten thousand words in an unknown tongue." We need to note two things here: the first is that Paul did indeed possess this gift and the second is that he rated it as being of comparatively little importance in the life of the Church compared with other gifts. What Paul puts last so many others today are putting first. I find it very difficult to understand why. *Why* this particular gift? Why do they stress it so much? Why do they look on it as apparently the most desirable thing for a Christian to possess while Paul says he would rather speak five words with his understanding than ten thousand words in an unknown tongue? Surely Paul is right, and if Paul is right then these dear people must be quite wrong. Finally we must note:

C. *The restraint which must rule us* in our approach to the study of this gift. And here are two final lines of thought which should exercise a restraining effect upon our whole approach:

(i) *The concern that should motivate me* in exercising the gifts of the Spirit. In 1 Corinthians 12:7 Paul lays down that the purpose of the exercise of the gifts of the Spirit is the profit of all: the enrichment, the equipment, the encouragement, the enlightenment of the total life and testimony of the fellowship. In this context, in the light of the fact that speaking in tongues is primarily an offering of praise to God by the individual, this gift obviously plays a minor and somewhat more individual-istic role. So in 1 Corinthians 14 there runs right through the chapter a stress on the need for edification and for understanding, and therefore a marked preference for the gift of prophecy which is not so much a foretelling of events as a forth-telling of God's truth. The Old Testa-ment prophets were not always foretelling what was going

64

to happen, they were speaking God's Word to God's people at a given time. Paul reckoned that the gift of preaching or communicating the Word of God was far more important than that of speaking with tongues. We see this brought out most vividly in chapter 14:1–5. This is something that Paul applies all the way through— firstly to fellowship among believers and secondly to witnessing to unbelievers (verses 22 to 25). Understanding and edification, conviction and conversion, not through the speaking with tongues but through prophesying, not a foretelling but a forth-telling of the Word of God. This is the motivation of true Christian love which is deeply concerned for others. From the concern that should motivate me, I turn to:

(ii) *The control that should regulate me* in exercising the gifts of the Spirit. In verse 33 Paul reminds the Corinthian Church that the God we worship is not the author of confusion but of peace, and in verse 40 again he says, "Let all things be done decently and in order." In my personal life and in my fellowship with other believers I am to exercise a control, or rather allow the Holy Spirit to exercise His control. So regulations are imposed to ensure that the real purpose for which the gifts have been given are achieved. In the fellowship of the Church there is to be *no* speaking with tongues *without* interpretation (verse 28) and if there is one to interpret then a limit is imposed on how many should be allowed to speak with tongues—two or three (verse 27). There must not be a "take-over" by those who claim to have this gift, and apparently in this respect some of the women were the worst offenders (verse 34)!

There are some people who seem to think that rules and plans curtail what they would like to call the freedom and the liberty of the Spirit but I don't find that here. What some people call "the liberty of the Spirit" I would be inclined to call "the laziness of the flesh" and when some people want to leave everything to what they are pleased to call the leading of the Spirit of God they could so easily make that a cover for excusing their own laziness. I like to think that I can have the leading of the Spirit of God in my study just as much as in my pulpit. I cannot imagine that the Holy Spirit of God is going to bless a laziness which refuses to study and prepare, and to seek to know the mind and will of God. The leading of the Holy Spirit now, for tomorrow if need be, is just as possible as His leading tomorrow itself. I will not get tomorrow's *grace* today—that is clear. God's grace is a present experience in its sufficiency. But I can get God's *guidance* today for tomorrow, if not His grace. So there will be a control that will regulate my exercise of the gifts of the Spirit.

Let us then hold these three lines of thought in balance. The reasons which must prompt me; the records which must guide me; the restraints which must rule me in my approach to this gift of the Spirit, which Samuel Chadwick says comes in the *last* place, and that surely is the *best* place in our thinking, in our aspiring, in our attaining! One of the great missionary societies in the United States summed up its policy and attitude towards this particular gift in four words: "Seek not, forbid not." So don't listen to Christians who claim to be speaking in harmony with the teaching of the Bible when they tell you that you ought to have this gift or they tell you that you cannot be filled with the Spirit without it. *That is just not true.*

And to any Christians who might be tempted to take

up that attitude I would warn them that if by any chance *our* understanding and interpretation of the Scriptures of truth is correct and that therefore their interpretation is wrong, then they are not speaking by the Spirit at all, not by the Spirit of God that is. There is only one other spirit by which they can be speaking and that is the spirit which our Lord rebuked when Simon Peter said something to Him that was quite out of harmony with the mind and truth and purpose of God. You remember our Lord said to Simon Peter, "Get thee behind me, Satan." We need to remember that Satan can use Christians just as much as he can use those who are not. To propagate error is to do the work of Satan, and such voices and such words come not from Heaven but from Hell!

8 Failures in our relationship to the Holy Spirit

ACTS 4:18–5:11

I want to remind you that the possession of power always brings with it the possibility of peril. Recently, I was able to find time to go down to Prestwick where my younger son, Henry, was completing his training as a pilot with BEA to fly Trident 3s. I arrived in time to see this magnificent aircraft flying round and round Prestwick Airport, landing on each circuit, going along the runway and then, with the tremendous roar of its engines, taking off again without stopping. To me it was incredible to think that a young man of 24 years of age was at the controls of such a concentration of power. The machine was costly, the power was tremendous and all of it under the control of a young man. A mistake could mean a costly disaster, both as far as machine and also as far as passengers were concerned although, fortunately, in training the plane carries no passengers. But three million pounds worth of costly material and engineering skill was at stake!

The promise to the Christian is the promise of the power of the Holy Spirit and the very possession of that power brings with it the possibility of peril. I want to pinpoint four kinds of failure that are specifically mentioned in the New Testament concerning the relationship of the believer to the Holy Spirit. Some have been hinted at already in our studies and are now brought together. These involve four Scripture references and the first comes in Acts 5:3 where we read of the Christian "lying" to the Holy Spirit. This I have called the failure of:

A. *Our dishonesty in the loyalty we have professed as Christians.* The incident was a dramatic one and it had two sides to it. First there was:

(i) *The movement of the Spirit of God.* Things were happening in the fellowship of the church in Jerusalem in spite of the opposition recorded and because of the intercession offered (cf. 4:24). The presence and the power of the Spirit of God was evident among the believers in a very noticeable way. In verse 33 we read of "great power" and "great grace." Part of what was experienced was seen in an overwhelming spirit of sacrificial giving which we read of in verse 34 following. And so these three tremendous characteristics, three evidences of the presence and power of the Holy Spirit, were to be seen on every hand—power, grace and love. Of course, in these kinds of circumstances certain people became prominent because of what they did and above all, apparently, because of how they gave. This kind of situation can still happen in the life of any Christian fellowship where the power of God is experienced, where grace, power and love take over and dominate all life's relationships. We can also see here:

(ii) *A judgment of the servant of God.* Wherever you get the genuine article you get the counterfeit; and so it was at this time. Ananias and Sapphira, his wife, did two things they had every right to do. Following the example of others they sold some of their possessions. Differently from others, but with a perfect right to do it, they kept back part of the price. We read of this in chapter 5:1 and 2. But then things went wrong, because when they brought their gift to the Apostles which represented only a part of what they had obtained from selling their possessions, they pretended that they had given it all. It was a deliberate lie intended to conceal a deliberate act. It was a lie which Simon Peter said was not spoken to men but to the Holy Spirit and therefore to God Himself. The judgment was simply this—they were removed by God from the fellowship of the Church. Being Christians, of course, they went to be with Christ but they were no longer seen and no longer active in the life of the fellowship of the church in Jerusalem.

We can see here two things with which we should be concerned—two questions to which we need to find the answer. The first concerns: *What were their motives* and, therefore, what are our motives in our service for God? The impression we get is that Ananias and Sapphira wanted a prominence that would gain appreciation and even applause from men. And how subtly this motive can creep into our service. We want appreciation and even applause from other Christians for what we are, and what we do, and how we speak. The other question we want to ask is *What is the meaning of this incident?* What light does it shed upon our service for God? Surely simply this—that God has no place for those who seek their own. In this old story the removal was physical and dramatic: both Ananias and Sapphira died. Maybe there had to be this kind of lesson for the Church which was so young and could so easily have been spoiled so soon. Today the removal may not be a physical one. We may remain in the fellowship, we remain in office but the removal is a spiritual one. God ceases to use us, God ceases to bless. We are, as it were, crossed off God's lists of usable and trustworthy Christians and we are put on the shelf. The sin of lying to the Holy Spirit is a perilous possibility in the field of failure in our relationship to this divine person. (In passing, I want simply to mention that all this, of course, has nothing whatever to do with that other sin, the sin of an unbeliever, of blaspheming against the Holy Spirit—the sin that is called "the unpardonable sin" that no Christian could ever commit.)

The second reference is found in Ephesians 4:30 where we read of the possibility of a Christian "grieving" the Spirit, where Paul writes, "And grieve not the holy Spirit of God, whereby ye are sealed unto the day of redemption." Here we have the second area of failure; what I have called:

B. *Our disobedience to an authority we should obey.* Dr. Graham Scroggie has a helpful comment to make on what being sealed with the Spirit, which is relevant to the grieving of the Spirit, really means. He writes, "It is significantly interesting that this reference is in the letter to the Ephesian church. Ephesus was a seaport and there was a great trade in timber. Timber merchants went to Ephesus and purchased the timber but they could not always take it away with them at once. It had to be floated later to its destination. But when they purchased the timber they put their mark on it, the mark of appropriation, of possession, of ownership. It was theirs and remained theirs until it was finally redeemed."

Behind this perilous possibility of grieving the Holy Spirit, who is divine and infinite and eternal love, lies the fact that we, too, have been purchased and possessed. Do you remember how the hymn-writer puts it: "Then on each He setteth His own secret sign: 'They that have my Spirit, these' saith He, 'are mine.' " How do we "grieve" this Holy Spirit? Surely it is by failing to allow Him to

71

do in us that for which He has been given, by not being willing for Him to be active in our lives! It is by failing to allow Him to be in us that which He wants to be, by living lives which are not worthy of the name that we bear. Let us define these aspects of this one sin. First there is:

(i) *The unwillingness that is shown by us.* It is as if the owner of a house has appointed a servant to look after his house and carry out his wishes but when the owner comes and wants to do this or that in his own home, to go here or there, the servant frustrates his every move, his every declared intention. The servant stands continually in his way, blocking his advance, forbidding him to do this, forbidding him to do that. What an absurd situation! What a ridiculous position for the owner, and for the servant. But this is just what can happen in the life of a Christian who has been purchased and possessed. The loving Spirit is, of course, the owner: describing Him as the seal indicates ownership and possession. We are but the servants, the occupants of a house that is owned by someone else, but so often we will not allow Him to do what He wants to do. What it is that the Holy Spirit wants to do we have seen already in an earlier study. How much there is that He does want to do in the life of every Christian through His *ministries,* as I call them to distinguish them from the *gifts* of the Spirit. When He comes and asks to be allowed to do in our lives what He has been given to do, we forbid Him! This unwillingness shown by us can grieve the Holy Spirit. Secondly, there is:

(ii) *The unworthiness that is seen in us.* This can grieve the Holy Spirit. Here again the analogy of the owner of the house comes in useful. The Holy Spirit not only wants

72

to do certain kinds of things, he wants to be a certain kind of person. So it is for the owner to decide the purposes for which all the rooms are to be used, not the occupant or servant; the way the rooms are to be furnished, what they will contain. The room and the contents would then reflect the character of the owner, his attitudes and his attributes. Supposing the servant brushed all these aside, supposing he brought in everything that *he* wanted to have there, turning this room into a cocktail bar, plastering the walls of another with obscene pictures? Anybody coming in would be horrified. Is this what we do? Are we content to be the kind of people we are, whose characters bear no resemblance to that of the Holy Spirit to whom we belong? So unworthiness seen in us by others can grieve the Holy Spirit.

We want to be what *we* want to be. We want to do what *we* want to do. This is our disobedience to an authority we should obey.

The third reference to failure in the relationship of the believer to the Holy Spirit is found in 1 Thessalonians 5:19 where Paul warns against the sin of "quenching" the Spirit. "Quench not the Spirit." For a long time I used to puzzle over this. Was Paul simply saying over again the same thing as he had said in his letter to the Ephesian Church? Or was he saying something different? Then this thought came to me which seemed to throw light upon this verse. Is it possible that, while grieving the Spirit has primarily reference to my relationship to the Holy Spirit in me, quenching the Spirit primarily has reference to the Holy Spirit in others? This suggests the third heading: the sin of failure through:

C. *Our disparagement of an activity we have discerned,* an activity, that is, of the Holy Spirit in the lives of others.

73

We then set out deliberately to bring all that activity to a halt; or maybe we don't do it deliberately but unintentionally. The word "quench" is always used in connection with fire, and fire you will recall is a symbol of the character of God and was also one of the signs that accompanied the coming of the Holy Spirit at Pentecost, as well as part of the promise in the prophecy of John the Baptist concerning the ministry of our Lord. Let us consider then:

(i) *What the fire will do.* When the fire of the Holy Spirit begins to burn in a life there are at least three things that will immediately be evident:

(*a*) the fire will burn out all that is unworthy. The Holy Spirit refines and reveals in a life in which He is active that which is unworthy of Christ. There is immediately an awareness of what should not be in the life and this is linked with an abandonment of what is unworthy. And so young Christians begin to alter their ways, their habits. Things begin to go out of their lives; they drop certain things that previously they did without question. The fire will burn out all that is unworthy.

(*b*) the fire will also burn in all that is praiseworthy. If we take the analogy of the potter and the vessel (a symbol of what we are in the hands of God) we realize what a crucial part the fire plays in the work of the potter. The colours and the design are all made permanent and glorious by the fire. In the story of a visit, I think by Dr. Stewart Holden, to a pottery works, he noticed that the potter preparing the vessel for the flames and heat of the oven was putting on a lot of black with his transfers. Dr. Holden commented on this, to which the potter replied, "When it comes out of the fire the black will have turned to gold." So, in the life of the Christian, not only

74

do some things go out but others come in: new interests, new standards, new ambitions, new motives. The whole life becomes beautiful in colour and design, and all this is the result of the activity of the Holy Spirit.

(c) the fire will also burn through. Fire has tremendous penetration. Sometimes we have seen workmen cutting through a massive steel girder with a burning flame. A life can begin to count for God when that life, in which the Holy Spirit burns fiercely, can burn through indifference, through hostility, through prejudice, through resentments. The fire of the Spirit has begun to burn: light, heat and warmth. The fire of God is glowing in the life.

But just a word of warning—the fire must be the fire of the Spirit. In the Old Testament we read of "strange fire" with which some of the sons of Aaron transgressed and this brought upon them the sentence of death. Again, we are reminded of the possibility of a counterfeit and this possibility cannot be ignored. If the fire be that of the Spirit of God, however, we have seen some of the things it will do. Let us also note:

(ii) *How the fire is damped.* Fire can burn brightly or smoulder. The suggestion here is that we can sin against the Holy Spirit in the lives of others by pouring water on the fire of the Spirit in their lives; by destroying, by our discouragement, all that the Holy Spirit is trying to do; by reversing all that the Holy Spirit has initiated; by bringing to nothing and to an end the response of the heart to the Holy Spirit's initiative and action; by ridicule; by criticism; by discouragement. So we can pour buckets of water upon the fire in order to quench it.

Another way in which a fire can be damped down is not simply by pouring water on it but by putting too

75

much fuel upon the fire. We can quench the Spirit by demanding what the Spirit does not demand, by laying down our own conditions of blessing, by issuing our own commands, laying down our own obligations that are not in the Scriptures. We can put a fire out, or very nearly out, by putting far too much on it. The result is the same. Discouragement and the quenching of the Spirit in the lives of others.

The final reference is in 1 Timothy 4:14 where we see the perilous possibility of "neglecting" the gift of the Spirit given to us. The nature of the gift is irrelevant, the manner in which the gift has been received will vary but the simple danger is that of neglecting it. I have called this the sin of:

D. *Our dissipation of the energy we should conserve.* Neglect does not necessarily mean idleness. In an ordinary life a housewife can be busy all day long at Bingo and neglect her family; a husband can be busy all day long at business or on the golf course and neglect his wife; a Christian can be intensely busy in the life and activity of the Church and neglect his studies. What then is the lesson learnt here? First there is:

(i) *The need for having discernment.* We need to know what the gift is that God has given to us. Every Christian has a charisma, a gift; every Christian born again of the Spirit of God, indwelt by that same Spirit is a charismatic Christian. This we have seen in an earlier study. We have to find out what gift God has given to us and be content with that and not endlessly spend our time desiring, coveting, striving after another gift. Finally there is:

(ii) *The need for being diligent.* We are not to neglect this gift, we are to use it to the full and see that the gift God has given us is exercised diligently and faithfully.

So we come back to the picture with which we began this study, of a Trident 3 taking off from the runway at Prestwick Airport and at the controls a lad of 24, and in that massive machine costing three million pounds there is packed power enough to transport many passengers at six hundred miles an hour through space. What tremendous possibilities there are in such power but what tragic possibilities, too, for a blunder could lead to disaster. The same is true of the Christian—it is not enough to have the Holy Spirit; we must see that there is no failure in our relationship to Him.

9 Make love your aim

1 CORINTHIANS 13

In our final study we come back to those three chapters in the First Epistle of Paul to the Corinthians in which he was dealing with a situation at Corinth where, amongst other things, a distorted evaluation of the gift of speaking in tongues was obviously causing grave concern to Paul and confusion in the church. In chapter 12 Paul had dealt with the basic truths underlying his approach to the subject of "the gifts of the Spirit" in general. In chapter 14 he concentrated upon the one gift, the stress upon which was throwing the life of the church at Corinth out of balance, namely the gift of tongues. Chapter 12 ends with the words, "yet shew I unto you a more excellent way" and that more excellent way was the way of love as set out in chapter 13. Then chapter 14 opens with the words, "Make love your aim" (RSV)—not what you have been making your aim, namely the gift of speaking in tongues, but this more excellent way, the way of love.

We want to try and find out what this more excellent way is within the context of a false evaluation of the importance of one particular gift and a failure to understand that gifts of all kinds were given by the Holy Spirit for the building up of the fellowship in the faith. The more excellent way, the thing we are to make our aim, is the way of love—that love which is the fruit of the Spirit (Galatians 5:22), that love which has been "shed

78

abroad in our hearts by the Holy Ghost which is given to us" (Romans 5:5).

This thirteenth chapter of 1 Corinthians would seem to me to fall into three divisions: the importance of love (verses 1–3), the excellence of love (verses 4–7) and the permanence of love (verses 8–13). And from a consideration of these three aspects of love Paul claims that it is the more excellent way which we are to make our aim. Let us consider then:

A. *The importance of love* (verses 1–3). Here there are two points of view set out which produce a marked contrast. First of all we see what I have called:

(i) *The impressive achievements that man seeks.* Paul draws up a list of gifts and deeds which one would have thought wholly commendable and biblically desirable. He begins and starts his argument from the point at issue in the church at Corinth, namely the speaking in tongues, although the application of this reference could, of course, be extended to any kind of oratory. Then in verse 2 he notes certain other gifts of the Spirit which are of unquestioned value: the gift of prophecy, which approximates to that of preaching, a forth telling of the Word of God to men; the gift of spiritual insight and understanding; the gift of knowledge of the Word of God and of the ways of God; and finally the gift of faith. All of these are eminently commendable and eminently desirable. To that list of "gifts of the Spirit" he adds two other highly commendable and worthy attributes or activities of a Christian life within the fellowship and service of Jesus Christ. The first is that of generosity concerning our material possessions and the second a sacrificial way of living that was prepared even to accept death and martyrdom if need be. Paul has no fault to find

79

with any of these as such, but he looks at these same achievements from another point of view, that which I have called:

(ii) *The decisive assessment that God makes*. We discover that God is not so much concerned with *what we have*, or even with *what we do* with what we have, but *why we do* what we do with what we have. In other words, the divine assessment has more to do with the performer himself than his performance. The *motive* is what determines the worth and value of the use made of the gifts bestowed by God or dispersed by man. The mere exercise of the gifts may tell us nothing, the nature of the motive will tell us almost everything. And the divine assessment is pretty shattering. In the absence of divine love as a motivating principle the speaking with tongues becomes as meaningless and as valueless as the hideous clamour of gongs being beaten and cymbals clashing. The possessor of the gifts referred to in verse 2, if destitute of the motivation of divine love, gets no marks at all for his performance—a sobering thought for all of us who claim to speak with spiritual insight in the name of Christ. God does not evaluate the worth of what I say by an investigation into the message I preached but into the motive I had when I preached it. And as for the man who thinks of adding to his reputation as a Christian whether by material generosity or even a martyr's death, the addition to his reputation as far as God is concerned is precisely nothing unless the motivation is that of divine love. The point is, of course, that all these gifts can be used for motives that are utterly unworthy. Those gifts can be dispensed to the poor for motives that care little for the recipient and less for the good name of the Lord but are concerned simply for the reputation of the one distributing the gifts.

The importance of love is simply this, it is the only motive that gives any value to the use made of the gifts we have used, the possessions we have shared, the sacrifices we have borne. God's evaluation is concerned with motivation; the assessment is not so much an assessment of the performance as of the performer. It would almost be true to say that God doesn't care tuppence what gifts you have but He is concerned with how and why you use that gift, hence the importance of love. Then secondly let us consider:

B. *The excellence of love* (verses 4–7). I like Moffat's translation here. It reads: "Love is very patient, very kind. Love knows no jealousy; love makes no parade, gives itself no airs, is never rude, never selfish, never irritated, never resentful; love is never glad when others go wrong, love is gladdened by goodness, always slow to expose, always eager to believe the best, always hopeful, always patient."

It is interesting to note that this amazing list of the qualities that combine to portray the excellence of love all have to do with human relationships that exist in the practical, down-to-earth business of daily living, and surely it is here that the real crunch comes. What we are in the fellowship and worship of a community of believers is one thing but how we fare in the rough and tumble of the world can be quite another. I may be a preacher, and an excellent preacher, but God is not just concerned about my preaching. He may be more concerned about my temper! I may have the gift of tongues with which to speak to God in praise and worship and adoration, but what about the tongue with which I speak to my boss or the way in which I speak to my mother! And so it is in this area of human relationship that the excellence of love proves its worth. The possession of one or another of the gifts of the Spirit may have little effect here. Let us note:

(i) *The vices that love would discard.* The first that is named is *envy,* that spirit that grudges to another something it seeks for itself. A souring, embittering spirit that smoulders like a fire. That spirit that resents it when another gets promotion instead of itself: a spirit that is obsessed with seeking what it is never meant to have. The second vice that is named is *conceit;* "love makes no parade, gives itself no airs." Love knows nothing of the spirit that is always demanding attention, that must be given position whether or not (and usually not) either the attention or position are merited, deserved or earned! Love is content to serve by stealth without thanks and without praise. The third vice that is named is that of *rudeness.* The AV reads: "Doth not behave itself unseemly." Moffatt translates: "love . . . is never rude." There is a courteous consideration of the feelings of others so that neither in deed nor word is offence caused or injury inflicted. Love is always thoughtfully considerate. Can you imagine a fellow saying that he loved a girl and then being rude to her? It is unthinkable. The fourth vice is what I have called *selfishness,* which is a disinterest in others in the pursuit of its own interest, an absorption with itself. This is the very negation of love, which is always utterly unselfish. The AV here reads: "seeketh not her own" and RSV: "love does not insist on its own way"; the NEB translates: "love is . . . never selfish." The fifth vice is *touchiness* or irritability; the AV translates. "is not easily provoked" and the RSV: "love is not . . . resentful." J. B. Phillips has: "love . . . is not touchy" and the NEB: "not quick to take offence." What a lot of difficulties are caused by touchiness but love has more to do than to be bothered with such trivialities.

I have never forgotten a statement made by a Mr. Calder who trained us as young men and formed us into a hand-bell team. When he commenced his training with us he stated that he had two rules that he wanted to make plain. The first was that he never intentionally gave offence, and the second was he never took offence! What a wonderful stand to take. There was nothing of irritability or touchi-ness about him and he didn't want it in us.

The sixth vice is that of having *a good memory for in-juries received.* The AV translates it here that love "thinketh no evil." The word used for "thinketh" is a word used for the keeping of accounts. They say that an elephant never forgets; if that be true then some unloving Christians must surely have elephant blood in them somewhere—they never do forget and they specialize in not forgetting or forgiving injuries received! They are always suspicious of the motives of others; they are always careful to note blunders and injuries received by them. But here love again has bigger things on hand than to keep that kind of account. The last vice I have called *malice.* We read that love "rejoiceth not in iniquity, but rejoiceth in the truth." Love knows nothing of that malicious spitefulness that is glad when others go wrong and is even sorry if extenuat-ing circumstances are discovered which decrease the mea-sure of blame. This is the sin of the gossip, the defamer, the destroyer of reputations but true love knows nothing of all this. These are some of the vices discarded by love and running through this section also we can see:

(ii) *The virtues displayed by love*—and what lovely vir-tues they are. In verse 4 we read of *patience.* "Love" translates Moffatt "is very patient," and the word used indicates the thought is that of patience with people. How true this is of love. Think of the patience of a mother with her child, the child who keeps crying, the child who will not eat, the child who is wilful, wayward and rebellious. The patience of love that keeps on trying to understand, trying to guide, trying to influence, trying to help. Then we have *kindness* "Love" says Paul "is very kind." There is a gentleness in the manner of love. Love is sensitively afraid lest it should hurt the one loved, and with rare insight and tenderness will always be thinking out how it could please; what would please; trying to understand, trying to avoid doing anything that might hurt. How desperately we need kindness in this unkind world— thoughtful consideration of others. In verse 7 we have *endurance*. Love does not easily give in or give way or give up: love holds out and holds on. And then we have *confidence*. "Love" Paul says "believeth all things." It is always prepared to believe the best and therefore so often gets the best from people. Next we have *hopefulness*. Even when all grounds for confidence seem to have gone love still hopes. How often one sees this pathetically demonstrated in a home where, maybe, a husband is an alcoholic but the wife still loves the sodden wretch she calls her husband, and because she loves she hopes. Although her hopes have been dashed again and again to the ground, she still hopes on that one day, maybe, the curse will leave her husband's life and the chains of this terrible habit that enslaves him will be broken. And finally we have *persistency*. Love just keeps on loving, keeps on doing what it knows has to be done even if its heart is breaking, even if the tears flow in the secret place, even if the effort seems too great, love struggles on. It will not allow itself to be discouraged or diverted or dismissed.

The excellence of love is seen in the vices it discards and in the virtues it displays. What an excellence this is! No wonder St. Paul speaks of it as a better way; no wonder he tells the Christians at Corinth to make this their aim. If only we could be convinced of this; that this is something greater than any gift of the Spirit, this fruit of the Spirit which is love; this love which has been shed abroad in our hearts; this love which, if it permeated all the human relationships of life, would transform life in a much deeper, richer, more wonderful way than the possession of any gift—let alone the gift of speaking with tongues upon which the Corinthians laid such great store. I have heard Christians praying for many things; I don't know whether I have ever heard them praying for love.

From the importance and excellence of love, we turn, finally, to:

C. *The permanence of love* (verses 8–13). Let us remind ourselves of the context, that Paul is dealing with the strains and stresses in the thinking of the Christians at Corinth because of the overrated evaluation they put on certain gifts of the Spirit. The final argument that Paul uses in this section has to do with the truth of the permanence of love and the transiency of the gifts they value so highly. We can see in these closing verses, first:

(i) *The illustrations that Paul uses.* The illustration of growing up, in verse 11, where he points out that so much that played a part in childhood becomes irrelevant in adult life. So much that may have seemed important to us in our childhood here on earth is seen to be irrelevant in the light of the life to come. He uses the illustration, too, of journeying on from this life to that which is to come when we pass from one scene to another. There is much that is of temporary value in both these earlier experiences;

85

but then things that were of temporary value end with having no value at all. And in this category Paul puts the gifts of the Spirit which did have a part to play in our lives as Christians but have no permanent place in our experience. There will be no tongues in Heaven, he says, for "tongues ... shall cease." There is going to be no preaching in Heaven! What a thought for those of us who are preachers and ministers that the very thing upon which we have spent all our strength and so much of our time will cease to be relevant and will not exist when this life on earth is over. And no-one will be able to claim a greater knowledge than anybody else of God Himself in Heaven, because we will know Him then as He knows us now. These are the illustrations that Paul uses to indicate the fact that things of value have a way of losing their value, but that there are some things which retain their value through life on earth and through all eternity to come. There is also:

(ii) *The applications that Paul makes.* Besides the things that are of partial or passing value there are things of permanent value and therefore logically and sensibly and spiritually he says that our concern should be with them. And finally he names three qualities that are of permanent and abiding value. He writes : "Now abideth faith, hope charity (love), these three; but the greatest of these is love." The permanence of love. One of the sad things about so many Christians is that they are setting great store by things that are not permanent; by things that will cease; by things that will become irrelevant; things that may serve a purpose, albeit a very modest purpose, during our life here on earth, and all the time we are neglecting the things that will remain and abide through time and through eternity.

Is it any wonder then that Paul calls "love" the more excellent way? Is it any wonder that he says to these Christians whose insights have got all mixed up, whose evaluations are all wrong, "Make love your aim"? What a transformation could come over the life of every church if every Christian followed Paul's counsel and advice.

This seems to me a worthy note upon which to end these studies on "The Person and Work of the Holy Spirit in the Life of the Believer." The fruit of the Spirit is love. The love of God has been shed abroad in our hearts by the Holy Spirit given to us, therefore ... MAKE LOVE YOUR AIM.

Tape recordings of these Bible Studies as originally given are available from the Christian Book Centre, 1021 Argyle Street, Glasgow G3 8LZ.